How Can I Help?

Printed in the United States

Aspen Books, 6208 S. Stratler, Murray, UT 84107

Library of Congress Cataloging-in-Publication Data

Bennion, Lowell Lindsay
How can I help? : final selections by the legendary writer, teacher, and humanitarian / Lowell L. Bennion.
p. cm.
ISBN 1-56236-229-1
1. Christian life—Morman authors. I. Title.
BX8656.B465 1996
248.4'89332—dc20 96-12054
CIP

HOW CAN I HELP?

LOWELL L. BENNION

FINAL SELECTIONS BY THE LEGENDARY
WRITER, TEACHER, AND HUMANITARIAN

• • • • •

Foreword by Emma Lou Thayne

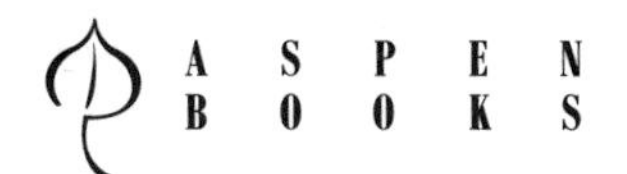

Contents

Foreword

Live life to the fullest. " . . . not to be downhearted . . . in whatever misfortunes may befall me—This is life; this the task of life. . . This idea has entered into my flesh and blood."

Dostoyevsky, Letter to his brother
Lowell L. Bennion
I Believe, p. 36

February 21, 1996, Lowell Bennion died at home of Parkinson's disease. He was eighty-seven. In his passing a guiding light went out in the broad community fed by him both physically and spiritually. He would have deprecated the attention paid by newspapers, television, radio, and thousands of friends sorrowed by his passing. Awards, his name in headlines, buildings or centers named for him were to him an embarrassment.

Recently when asked if he had any idea how many people he had influenced, he smiled and said, "I don't have time to think about that." Of course not. He was too busy attending to the well-being of everyone else. The biggest question for those of us he taught and befriended is, What kind of world will this be without Lowell? Who to speak for the disenfranchised, look out for the needy, counsel with the questioners, laugh with us over mis-steps, and commiserate with us over losses? Who to build bridges and cultivate peace? Who to celebrate our own faith even in respecting the faith of others? Who with enough bigness to champion the littlest of us? Whoever so inclusive, so loving, so loved? I believe he would wish us simply to ask as he did, "How can I help?"

October brisk, a day in 1987 I remember clearly. Lowell Bennion, seventy-nine, drives the streets of Salt Lake's central city as if the neighborhood were his own. He is delivering a box of food to eighty-two-year-old Mrs. Strouder just out of cataract surgery and living alone. His passenger is my friend, a communist visitor from the Soviet Union. I get to watch. She has toured the Community Services food bank that he directs and asks now, "Where do the supplies come from?"

"From donations," he answers, eyes twinkling. His tweed sport coat and French tam, his huge hands on the wheel, the ruddiness of his cheeks all belie the encroaching impairment of arthritis and Parkinson's disease that prevent his raising his arms above his chest.

"And suppose the donations cease?" she asks, confused at the giving that she has never heard of in her country. "We do not have a word for 'donation' or for 'charity' in my language."

"They never do cease. People are always willing," Lowell says, with the same contagious assurance that he'd brought to a class or a book for more than sixty years. He would say, "For me, money is instrumental. A certain amount of it is essential for food, clothing, shelter, a measure of respectability, and some of the amenities of life such as enjoying the arts and offering hospitality. While I could use millions of dollars—not for personal, luxurious living, but for social projects which would enable the disadvantaged to find satisfying roles to play in our society—I do not believe in seeking money for its own sake, in lusting after it, or in possessing so much that I live in fear of losing it."[1]

Turning off State Street into a neighborhood that could challenge a social project, he points out, "There's where Mrs. Gillespy's daughter and her triplets live. The little ones are getting along a lot better this week. They're up to twelve pounds. There's Mr. Johnson trying to get his garbage out. I'm glad Jay next door is inclined to help him. Mrs. Strouder lives right up here, in that red brick bungalow. The kids from the Center painted the trim and the porch last week. But she's lonely. She came home yesterday to nobody after her cataract surgery. She's having a hard time."

"How do you know?" the Soviet visitor asks, taking notes, fifteen time zones and two ideologies away from home.

"We have a list of senior citizens, several hundred, at the Center. They're classified whether they have children, a husband or a wife, anybody, and whether they need food."

He pulls up to the curb in the little white Escort station wagon, winds down the window to the tailgate by pushing a button. "It's automatic," he smiles again. "Isn't it something? I'm spoiled. I don't have to do anything for myself."

The car was a gift from money raised to honor him for all the gifts he'd given. He'd been driving an old truck with manual shift and hard steering. He'd had great difficulty winding the windows up or down and an even harder time reaching into the bed to deliver what he'd been distributing in any weather.

Those who had raised the money said no one turned them down, in fact they said, "For Lowell Bennion? I'd give anything." Some even called in the night or came to the door with a check saying, "Am I too late? I want to be in on this!" Over five hundred donors, contacted in a week, only by word of mouth, gave monies which were matched by an automobile dealer friend to allow the purchase. It had been registered in Lowell Bennion's name before it got to him so he couldn't be tempted to give it away to anyone. The money that was left over would be put toward his biography. (Mary L. Bradford, *Lowell L. Bennion*, Dialogue Foundation, 1995.)

Mrs. Strouder meets them at the door, with a patch over one eye. "Oh, you dear Mr. Bennion you've come." Her living room hangs like her chenille bathrobe, dingy with old smells of urine and cats. She uses a cane to start toward the kitchen. "You'll have something to drink, Mr. Bennion? Water at least? And I'm happy to meet such a special guest—from Russia!"

Between sips of water, he asks and Mrs. Strouder talks of the pain, the loneliness. "But your box—it'll help a lot, Mr. Bennion. More than even you know." As he rises to go, she makes it to the door, pulls it open, shakes the hand of the Russian, hard, then, from inches above him, gives Mr. Bennion a hug.

He reddens, puts his tam back on the shining bald head, and says, "Just remember the box comes from lots of folks, people who care about you, Mrs. Strouder. Now you take care of you. We'll be in touch."

In touch. That's what Lowell's life was. A lifetime of being in touch, always in plurals: across faiths, cultures, races, ages, disciplines, languages, circumstances. Descriptions of him run to series after series: teacher, writer, counselor, humanitarian, scholar, brother, husband and father, outdoorsman, friend, man of God. Able to make us laugh, feel, be, do, he was in touch with the human condition, with people, aiding and comforting, challenging, making us think. He was the link, the interpreter, the catalyst.

Living life to its fullest—of course that was in his flesh and blood.

And essence. Body and spirit together. Soul. The ultimate communication. That's what Lowell Bennion trafficked in. Often an enigma to many operating in dogma or political savvy, he stayed himself, part of the land he loved to cultivate, the heads and hearts he loved to teach and learn from, the people he served. The gospel of Jesus Christ he spread as if opening a window to sunlight, his own earthy wisdom like a face in a Rembrandt painting, illuminated from inside.

That life lived to the fullest, what was it?

In 1933, the same year Hitler came to power, Lowell completed work for his Ph.D. at Strasbourg University in France. He was twenty-five. Fresh from three years as a Mormon missionary, he had studied in France and a Germany fomenting in pre-Nazism. He prepared his dissertation about German sociologist and philosopher Max Weber, studied for it in German, wrote it in English, and defended it in French. The paper alone might have catapulted him to a top-rank professorship in America where Weber was yet to be discovered. He would choose instead to become director of an LDS institute of religion for college students.

In Germany, he was a young husband. Married before his mission, together with his bride for only a month, then separated for nearly three years, he took a train from Germany and she a ship and a train from Utah to meet in Paris. On a pittance, they studied and traveled exultantly, had a baby girl who had red curly hair like his. In the same year he received his degree, their child died. Nineteen years later his closest brother died in an accident at thirty-three. In another nineteen years a four-year-old grandson died in his sleep. About each untimely death, and at the hundreds of funerals where he was chosen speaker, like Job he praised and never blamed his God.

For twenty-eight years, as a teacher and administrator he originated classes and programs, socials and worship services; danced, ate, laughed and cried with institute students; taught Christianity over Churchianity. Never without humor, he could find fun in dailiness. If a malaprop institute student wanted to write a paper on "The three degrees of immorality," he could counter with "Oh, that's my partner's area of expertise." He became beloved—and was relieved of his job. Why, no one ever explained,[2] yet Lowell was never bitter or vindictive. Two university presidents vied for his services before he moved on as a University of Utah associate dean of students and professor of sociology. At seventy he became director of Salt Lake Community Services and a bishop in the church he never stopped serving.

Flexible, he accepted change when warranted. He grew up rooted in tradition, wanted his wife, like his mother, to be in the home with their five children, thought he was protecting her in saying she was too precious to chance driving a car. Yet years later he chose free agency over orthodoxy and defended the Equal Rights Amendment on television in Utah.

As children will, his five came with their own luggage. He loved them in their diversity, as he did his students, friends, and those he worked with.

Knowing and always acknowledging the worth of each, he stood by them all equally in a lifetime of writing, teaching, and speaking for justice, mercy, and lovingkindness.

As early as the 1950s, in a day when being colored could crimp possibilities and create chasms of prejudice and prohibitions, this man chanced his position and spoke out for the rights of all, particularly black men banned until 1978 from the Mormon priesthood. In the 1990s, frail at eighty-three, he joined a candlelight vigil at the governor's mansion to plead for reprieve from the death penalty of an African-American man convicted of murder. From the crowd, his was still the opinion that television and newspapers sought to quote.

At a 1992 campaign dinner of "Democrats for Mike Leavitt [a Republican] for Governor," the crowd hushed as he entered, stooped and shuffling. "I never saw such reverence for anyone," said a young man who had never seen him before. Yet a decade earlier a man concerned with advertising and public relations had said after reading Lowell's remarks quoted in *Time* magazine, "That man knows nothing about P.R." Lowell's quote was the same as he'd lived by: "I can't believe in a religion that doesn't permit a person to use both his heart and his mind."

For more than fifty years he wrote books, manuals for the Church, texts, handbooks on the life of the spirit as it relates to the life of the mind and body. He wrote about friendship and marriage as well as scripture and service, was as eclectic in his learning as he was indefatigable in his contributing to a wider and wider pool of well-being.

All his days he dug in the earth, distributed produce, listened to Beethoven and read Goethe along with scriptures of diverse faiths. He masterminded all of it into service in places as varied as Central Salt Lake City and Mali, Africa. His Boys Ranch in the Idaho-Wyoming Tetons drew hundreds of youngsters for summers of learning to work, study, and play. In his name the Lowell L. Bennion Community Service Center at the University of Utah expected to put into action in 1995-96 as many as 6,000 students, faculty, and staff to serve people and causes with all over the valley.

Only physically did he change. His health—"tolerably good" according to him but drastically limited by any usual definition—brought falls and increasingly difficult recoveries. In his later years he had to give up driving—his shoulders that had lifted tons to thousands refused to work for him. But almost until the end of his life, students from the Bennion Center signed up to help him with his still imperative deliveries. He finally needed help to get a fork to his mouth, his vigorous body had so shriveled and weakened. But his mind and soul never did. Nor his resolve to stay real. And to be a furnisher.

Over more than fifty years as brother, bishop, professor, friend Lowell Bennion, as he had for countless others, offered consistent counsel to my constant asking: Should I go to graduate school with five teenage daughters, a husband, and a household to be in on? How might I write or speak for peace in a time of world turmoil? How can I champion the cause of free expression in the Church we both love, and still retain a Lowell Bennion faith in questing? His answers are the essence of what he taught:

Consider the overall benefit.
Overcome evil with good.
Be responsible for finding the full measure of your creation.
Act out of love, not fear or grievance.
Whatever you do, do with joy and with faith.
Keep you own voice, and write with your own pen.

In his eighty-fifth year, after a long visit with him and Merle[3] about what seemed unsolvable problems, I asked him to give me a blessing. I'd never asked before—only for advice. He gave me a blessing like no other I'd known. Since he couldn't raise his hands or stand steadily, I had to sit between his knees, facing out toward Merle, for him to reach to put his huge hands on my head. I felt the loving weight of them, like being engulfed by a magnet. Without a sign of the hesitation I'd come to expect in his speech, he gave me a blessing so private, so knowing, that I felt intimately connected to the Lord who has been with him forever. I will be alive to it as long as I live.

Lowell lives in the hearts of those who knew him—in person, in print, or by his works—like the Light that was his intimate companion. I say only what countless others have said or would like to say: Thank you, Lowell, my friend. For letting me know. And for this last book of essays—your own choices from a life lived to its fullest and always asking, "How can I help?"

Emma Lou Thayne
March 1996

1. *The Things that Matter Most*, Bookcraft, Salt Lake City, Utah, 1978, p. 25

2. *Lowell L. Bennion*, a biography by Mary L. Bradford, Dialogue, Salt Lake City, 1995, explains

3. Merle Colton Bennion died November, 1994

Introduction

As I have grown older, my appreciation of the complexities of life has deepened. I sympathize with those who struggle to find a good measure of satisfaction and joy. At best, we are all tested, sooner or later, during life's journey, and we must somehow learn to cope with what confronts us.

For some the journey is more difficult than for others. I am thinking of people with severe mental or physical handicaps. Then there are those who have the misfortune of being unwanted or unloved as little children or youths. Middle-aged people must struggle with earning a livelihood, rearing a family, and dealing with the problems of society. The elderly face disability and death, often alone. Living is easy for very, very few. And even when material and personal circumstances combine in gracious ways, all of us have challenges of the spirit. All of us grope to find our way and hope to face life with courage, faith, and wisdom.

Bookstores and libraries are filled with self-help books and articles, both scholarly and popular, offering ways to cope with the increasing stresses of modern life. So, why, one might ask, write another one?

Three emphases may justify this book. First, my concern is not with the nuts and bolts, or specific techniques and procedures for coping. I have chosen instead to identify attitudes toward life that hamper our adaptability and frustrate our search for acceptance that we might clearly avoid them. Two of these attitudes stem from seeking perfection and expecting to reap rewards from good actions. I have tried to apply religious principles to our ability to cope with everyday living. Too often religion is thought of largely in conjunction with theological beliefs and church activity. Both realms are meaningful, but religion should also help us live through each day. And through that living, we ought to experience a high degree of joy. I have also sought to offer guidelines for making life's biggest decisions, based on these same basic beliefs.

In the essays that follow, I suggest ideas that I have found helpful in meeting the challenges and vicissitudes of life. They have helped me; some may help you. At the very least, they may stimulate you to clarify and increase your own capacity to deal with life more creatively.

The first section deals with some basic principles that are critical to increasing our ability to serve and subsequently our level of satisfaction with life. In the second section I offer some practical advice to youth in regard to key decisions in life. The third treats more specific guidelines for coping with life's stresses. The fourth section addresses matters of the mind and spirit that affect how joyful our lives will be.

I believe this is a logical sequence. Before we can help a marriage partner or a child, we must get our own lives in reasonable order. My experience as a teacher, bishop, father, husband, and human being tells me that people who hate themselves do not love their neighbors but use and abuse them in a hopeless effort to lift their own egos.

It is my hope that reading this last little book of mine will not multiply problems or increase discouragement but will rather ease or eliminate burdens that we need not carry.

Life is a wonderful gift. I hope you can enjoy it as much as I have.

SECTION ONE

Building the Foundation for a Life of Service

Service, Self-Esteem, & the God-Centered Life

One of our most basic psychological needs is self-esteem, to have a feeling and an assurance of being a person of worth. We are so conscious of the self that we need to feel good about ourselves. How can we achieve this?

A very common, but ineffective, approach is to focus on things we can touch and see that we can identify with ourselves. Naturally we are concerned with our looks, height, weight, complexion, hair-style, teeth, glasses. Think of the time and money people spend to maximize their physical appearance.

Another way that supposedly enhances the self-image is multiplying possessions—a closet full of clothes, a sports car, a fine home with beautiful furnishings, a boat or a camper. We identify ourselves readily with the visible material things that surround us.

Except for attending to basic physical comforts and reasonable beauty in our surroundings, seeking self-esteem through external means has limited value because self-esteem comes from an internal feeling and awareness. Overblown externals are not intimately related to the inner psyche. All the efforts to become beautiful or to possess riches in abundance don't satisfy the inner person where life is experienced most immediately and continuously.

Jesus said, "Take heed, and beware of covetousness: for a man's life consisteth not in the abundance of the things which he possesseth" (Luke 12:15). Jesus understood that the kingdom of God is within us, not in things external to us. (See Luke 17:21.)

To have a good self-image a person must, like Job of old, hold fast to his integrity. We must have values and ideals that we believe in and live by. We must be true to ourselves and honest with others. The mind is a single dwelling, not a duplex or an apartment house. It craves unity and wholeness. It cannot be all things to all men.

Integrity gives a person inner strength and a sense of continuity. It makes for stability and cohesiveness in the inner life. A person of integrity recognizes himself in any and every circumstance.

Jesus gave us another important means to find our worth. "For whosoever shall save his life shall lose it; but whosoever shall lose his life for my sake and the gospel's, the same shall find it" (Mark 8:35). This sounds paradoxical but it is true. A self-centered life keeps us from knowing life in its fullness, at its best. To function fully and to experience life wholly, we must commit ourselves to a cause outside the self. Only then can we be whole and fully unified.

The best way to lose life for Christ's sake is to serve fellow beings. "By this shall all men know that ye are my disciples, if ye have love one to another"

(John 13:35). To make others happy by helping them to develop their human and divine potential is the best way I know to feel our own worth.

Truly, the kingdom of God is within us. It lies in our integrity, love, and other fine qualities of mind and heart. To cultivate the inner life is the way to self-fulfillment and the good life.

People who feel their own worth meet life from a position of strength. Such people are anchored, serene, and undisturbed by countless irritants which trouble those lacking inner strength. If we cultivate the kingdom of God within us—basing our own worth on the spiritual values of the gospel such as faith, humility, integrity, and love—we can cope with any and all of the corrupt kingdoms which make up our outside world.

In our prayers we usually petition the Lord for what we need—for health and strength, for protection of loved ones, for success in our work, for forgiveness of our sins. We become the focus of our own interest and the Lord the instrument of our help.

One of the most memorable prayers in my experience had a very different orientation. It was spoken by a college student at a Thanksgiving worship service and said something to this effect: "Lord, we usually come to thee asking for blessings. Today, we come only to thank thee for life, sunshine, friends, for thy word, thy love, for clothes to wear, food to eat, a home to live in. For thy bounteous gifts, too numerous to mention, Lord we thank thee this Thanksgiving season." It was a beautiful prayer that was God-centered rather than self-centered. It lifted us to a mood of adoration and worship.

I wonder if our lives are not much like most of our prayers, self-centered. Do we put ourselves center stage and expect all action to revolve around our own needs and desires?

How would it be to put God at the center of our lives instead of ourselves? Suppose we dedicated our desires and energies to seek and do his will instead of our own. "Lord, what would you have me do this day and in these circumstances?"

We would still go about our work in the morning or go to school, but it would be with the Lord's will and interest in mind. We would treat his children with respect and concern. We would feel gratitude for his gifts of life.

A friend of mine lived into his nineties, still youthful and serene. I asked him the secret of his well-being. He replied, "I never worry. If I have a problem, I go into my bedroom, close the door, and talk to the Lord. I lay the issue before him, put it on his shoulders and he guides me to a solution."

This approach would relieve us of much self-concern, worry, anxiety, and stress. St. Francis of Assisi expressed this thought beautifully:

> Lord, make me an instrument of your peace.
> Where there is hatred, let me sow love.
> Where there is injury, pardon.
> Where there is doubt, faith.
> Where there is despair, hope.
> Where there is darkness, light.

Where there is sadness, joy.
O Divine Master,
Grant that I may not so much seek
To be consoled, as to console,
To be understood, as to understand,
To be loved, as to love.
For it is in giving, that we receive,
It is in pardoning, that we are pardoned,
It is in dying, that we are born to eternal life.

A revelation in the Doctrine and Covenants is even more pointed in its God-centeredness.

> And if your eye be single to my glory, your whole bodies shall be filled with light, and there shall be no darkness in you; and that body which is filled with light comprehendeth all things.
>
> Therefore, sanctify yourselves that your minds become single to God, and the days will come that you shall see him; for he will unveil his face unto you, and it shall be in his own time, and in his own way, and according to his own will. (D&C 88:67-68)

Why Christian Love Means Service

One way to understand Christian love is to contrast it with two other kinds of well-known love: romance and friendship. What is unique about love of neighbor? How does it differ from romantic love or love between friends?

1. Christian love is alter-ego centered. Its whole concern is the well-being of others. It is unselfish and selfless. If self-concern enters the picture, it diminishes the quality of love.

By contrast romantic love is full of awareness of self. The romantic lover keenly senses his or her desire for another's affection and may become jealous of any competition for that affection. Romantic love tends to be self-centered, even as it seeks a return of the love it offers.

Love between friends, although quite unselfish, is a give-and-take (a mutual) relationship. Friends nourish each other and know what they can give and receive from their friendship. Friendship continues as both are fed in that relationship.

2. Christian love is universal. It includes all men and women and children—every person. This was the astounding new meaning Jesus gave to love in

the Sermon on the Mount:

> Ye have heard that it hath been said, Thou shalt love thy neighbour, and hate thine enemy.
>
> But I say unto you, Love your enemies, bless them that curse you, do good to them that hate you, and pray for them which despitefully use you, and persecute you;
>
> That ye may be the children of your Father which is in heaven: for he maketh his sun to rise on the evil and on the good, and sendeth rain on the just and on the unjust.
>
> For if ye love them which love you, what reward have ye? do not even the publicans the same?
>
> And if ye salute your brethren only, what do ye more than others? do not even the publicans so?
>
> Be ye therefore perfect, even as your Father which is in heaven is perfect. (Matt. 5:43-48)

By contrast romantic love and friendship are necessarily limited. Full romantic love is most genuine and meaningful when expressed between two people. Friendships are limited because of mutual attraction or indifference. Often there may also be a limit on time one can devote to friendship-building and maintenance. Christian love has no such impediments. One imbued with Christian love is willing to sacrifice any and all interests to meet the needs of others.

3. Christian love is unconditional. One need not earn it by repentance, reciprocation, or discipleship. The only question is, will my love in some measure meet the need of another human being?

Anyone who loves unconditionally will experience love, but the recipient of that love will likely not recognize it unless it satisfies some need. There are many needs that love can fulfill. Some are tangible, but others, just as real, are intangible.

TANGIBLE NEEDS

An increasing number of citizens in the USA are elderly, many over seventy-five and into their eighties and nineties. Women in this age group significantly outnumber the men. Many are poor and have very modest incomes. Add to these the disabled in our society, those crippled by disease or accident, and we find a large and increasing number of fellow citizens who need help.

Some lack the basic necessities of life: food, clothing, and shelter, including heat. If these people live in their own homes, much work is required to maintain them: weeding flower beds in spring, summer, and fall, washing windows, planting flowers and/or vegetables, painting the house or doing minor house repairs such as replacing screen doors and windows. When widows' husbands were well and alive they may well have rejoiced in their homes; now many of them have neither the strength to do the work nor the money to hire it done.

Inside the home, walls and windows need washing, and repairs often require skilled attention. One woman drained her kitchen waste water into a bucket under her sink for four years because she couldn't afford a plumber. Many homes lack bolt locks and smoke alarms to protect residents from robbers and fires. Neighbors, skilled and unskilled, and church and social groups could very easily provide the necessary help to people to maintain their homes inside and out.

Some people need help in getting dressed and undressed, getting into and out of bed, showering, preparing and serving simple meals. A woman in her eighties felt quite good but required these services to stay out of a nursing home. A willing neighbor in her fifties came in several times a day for just a few minutes and provided enough help to enable this elderly woman to remain in her home. She saw the need and fulfilled it without being asked or paid.

Many people, especially the elderly, have medical and dental problems. In the meantime if all doctors and dentists would donate ten percent of their time serving these individuals—as some do—much suffering could be relieved.

INTANGIBLE NEEDS

There are intangible needs which are just as real as the tangible ones we have named above. Moreover, they often require no special technical training to satisfy, but mainly Christian love and human understanding. Some of these intangible needs are:

1. To give and receive love—to feel accepted by other humans, to feel care and concern from and for others.
2. To feel creative or productive, that one is contributing to life and justifying one's existence.
3. To know self-esteem or a sense of one's own worth.
4. To have the feeling or faith that life is purposeful and hence meaningful.

Human beings are social as well as individual by nature. Our greatest psychological human need is to be accepted by other human beings, to give and receive love, to have affectionate security. I took a box of food from the Salt Lake Food Bank to an elderly widow one day. After a pleasant visit I said good-bye. She said with tearful eyes, "Mr. Bennion, come again, please, if only to say hello."

From the cradle to the grave, all people need someone to communicate with, someone to listen to them, hold their hands, show an interest in them. I marvel at the universality and the urgency of this human need for love and how Jesus made it the central, unifying principle of his gospel. When this love is understood and lived, it fulfills and satisfies human needs to a remarkable degree. There is no substitute for love in life, either in giving or receiving.

We humans were born to function. This is noticeable even in the life of an infant who kicks and cries, in the life of the curious and probing child, in the quest for independence of the adolescent, and in the searching life of the mature adult.

Ideally, we need to be creative in our self-expression. Creativity enhances self-esteem. We need not be a great artist, composer, or thinker to be creative. We must only find the courage, faith, and the know-how to express our own thoughts and actions.

Human beings are self-conscious. We not only act, but we reflect on our actions. We evaluate our behavior. We have a pressing need to make it acceptable in our own eyes. Much is said about our need for self-esteem or a feeling of our own worth. To have it to a reasonable degree is prerequisite to happiness.

To be aware of our creativity will enhance the feeling of self-worth more, I believe, than anything else. Other experiences help: To receive commendation for our actions, to have a feeling of growth in our abilities, to receive a promotion at work or a new assignment in the church or community.

We also need to find purpose and hence meaning in life as a whole. Each individual as a small part of a large universe and complex human existence has a need to make sense of life and find a place in it. I don't believe we are all accidents of the impersonal forces of nature. Rather, we are players on the earth created by an intelligent creator. To believe this means to believe that human creations of truth, goodness, and beauty—even death—are not at the mercy of nature. The things we cherish most have cosmic support from God.

When we meet people's needs with unconditional love, we (as well as the recipients of our love) are blessed. But love needs to be expressed intelligently to enhance the lives of others. To love unconditionally blesses the giver of love. To love with an understanding of the other person and in a way that satisfies in some measure his or her need blesses the recipient of our love.

HOW TO DEVELOP CHRISTIAN LOVE

If love is the most basic principle of the gospel and of life, we should do our utmost to develop this virtue. How can we increase our love of neighbor?

1. One way is to love ourselves. Not to love self may stand in the way of loving others. Yet, Christian love is alter-ego centered. To find the self, we must

lose it. Why then does love of neighbor presuppose love of self?

We have a great need to accept ourselves and to have a sense of our own worth. Only when we achieve this are we free to give our lives to others. In counseling I have learned that people with low self-esteem have a tendency to knock other people down to their level. Only when one is self-accepting, is he or she free to love others.

2. Another way is to love our neighbors in the name of Christ. A young Englishman couldn't decide whether to become a professional sportsman or a medical doctor. He finally decided on the latter course. When he graduated from medical school he had a choice—to work in a hospital in London or to go to sea with fishermen. He decided to go to sea. Having decided this, should he spend his home life in comfort in London or go where he was needed the most? He decided to spend his life in service.

He went to Labrador where there was a great need for medical service. He decided to go and to serve in the name of Christ. He let nothing interfere with his purpose or his work. He married a woman, a nurse, who shared his philosophy and joined him in his labors. Late in life he said, "The only regret I have is that I did not decide sooner to be a follower of Jesus."

I was privileged to meet Sir Wilfred. I have never looked into the face of a human being where I saw more joy and peace than I did in his. Walking in the path of Christ, seeking his Spirit to be with us, would certainly add motivation and a unique spiritual quality to our efforts to love others.

3. The surest way to develop Christian love is to practice it. This calls for concentration, for self-analysis, for repeated effort until it becomes spontaneous. Seek out people you know who need love and then give it to them. Opportunities abound. There are little children who need affection, adolescents who seek compliments and trust, older people who crave companionship and physical help.

We need to become more people-conscious. Examine our own lives. What are our needs? Might not others have the same needs? Could we not do unto others as we would have them do unto us?

These three ways of enhancing our ability to feel and express Christian love: increasing self-love, loving in partnership with Christ, and learning by doing, will keep our feet solidly on paths of satisfaction and joy.

Serving for the Right Reasons

To action alone has thou a right, not to its fruits." This Hindu proverb from Bhagavad Gita (Song Celestial) contains profound wisdom, offering a key remedy for removing stress from living.

No one lives in total isolation. Our actions lead us into relationships with nature, with other human beings, and with Deity. We cannot control their reactions and responses to our behavior except to a limited degree. To try to do so is futile.

The laws and forces of nature do not bend to my will. If I wish to get along with nature, I must learn its ways and adjust to them. Nature is quite indifferent to my needs and aspirations. But it helps when I understand and conform my behavior to natural laws. To make a simple analogy, my garden, whether planted with seeds, bulbs, or trees, will respond to the seasons. In spring it will bud then bloom. By fall it will be ready for late blooming or harvest. In winter leaves will fall and snow will strip it bare to lie dormant until another spring.

So I have tried to accommodate to aging and to all natural laws. Regardless of how we might wish to change the natural rhythms of muscle and bone fatigue, the assaults of disease or decay, our bodies and minds will weary and fail. For each it will be at a different rate and complexity. But it will happen. Our spirits, however, do not need to age.

I know a woman who in her eighties has failing eyesight after being a voracious reader all her life. She lives alone and spends most of her day in a mechanical chair that lifts her up and out of it so that she can move in her walker to her kitchen or bedroom. Still, she retains an enthusiasms for life. She listens to tapes of books and even newspapers. She watches informative TV shows and is a resource for ideas and quality opinions. She stays not only good company for others but for herself as well. She laughs often at the physical changes she is contending with. Of course sometimes she is discouraged, but she does what she can, stays in touch with God, and lets the days come as they will.

LDS apostle David O. McKay said to me when I began my teaching career, "Remember, words do not convey meanings, they call them forth." How true! I speak out of the context of my experience. People hear me out of the context of their feeling and thinking. No wonder communicating is difficult in marriage, in dialogue, on talk shows, and between nations. How can I hope to be understood by everyone, each hearing me from a different perspective?

Thus I live largely for the fruits of my actions; I put myself at the mercy of three powerful forces—nature, people, God—forces that are largely out of my control. Even fellow humans may not approve of my actions. They may be indifferent or simply unaware of my hopes and expectations. They may even put stumbling blocks in my way, rejecting or condemning my behavior with or without justifiable cause.

Nor can I expect the Lord to always do my bidding. I can ask and plead my cause, but he will certainly respond from his much wiser, more eternal perspective and not from my limited view of reality.

If, on the other hand, I act out of the conviction that what I am doing is right and worthwhile, no one can rob me of the satisfaction of living. My actions are under my control, and that makes it much easier to cope with my own convictions and actions than with the responses of others. These may differ radically from person to person and are subject to misinterpretation. Coping with oneself proves much simpler.

Concentrating on one's actions doesn't mean selfish living. My conduct may be as unselfish as I wish it to be. It just means that I don't live for my paycheck, awards, or other rewards, but mainly for the intrinsic satisfaction of what I do or how I behave.

Another reason I appreciate this Hindu saying is that it enhances integrity. It encourages me to act with singleness of purpose and keeps me from serving two masters. Jesus illustrated this point well in his Sermon on the Mount. He didn't promise gifts and rewards but simply recommended principles to live by. What we call "The Lord's Prayer" is supplication for the simplest of life's needs and protections along with praise for God who is the giver and forgiver of all.

> Our Father which art in heaven, Hallowed be thy name. Thy kingdom come. Thy will be done in earth, as it is in heaven. Give us this day our daily bread. And forgive us our debts, as we forgive our debtors. And lead us not into temptation, but deliver us from evil: For thine is the kingdom, and the power, and the glory, forever. Amen. (Matt. 6:9–13)

Doing things for their own sake is a richer experience than acting to please others. The basketball player who loves the game and plays it wholeheartedly will do better than one who plays for the plaudits of the grandstand. The speaker concerned with the response of his audience may be less effective than the one convinced of the importance of his message. The person who genuinely loves his neighbor will have a deeper experience than one who serves his neighbor hoping for a reward. He who pays tithing to open the windows of heaven for his own gain rather than to evidence his love of the Lord may have difficulty in maintaining the practice in hard times.

As a teacher, I frequently longed to communicate perfectly and powerfully my ideas of the gospel. How frustrated I felt if someone misunderstood me or—worse—seemed to understand but chose to follow another course than the one I advocated. At such times I found great comfort in remembering the advice of President McKay quoted earlier. I must find my reward as a teacher not in seeing my students fall into line behind me but in doing my absolute best in preparing my thoughts, presenting them clearly and sincerely, and listening to the experiences and thoughts of my students.

We must not, however, go to extremes on this issue. There are times when we *should* be interested in the fruits of our actions. We need to learn from our mistakes, improve our skills, and assess the value of our efforts. A teacher must know whether students understand the material presented; a conscientious surgeon should follow the progress of a patient; an architect should design a building that meets the needs of its occupants.

I am simply saying that we should concentrate on the rightness of our actions, on the value and meaning of what we are doing, and not look to the approval or praise of others for our reward. In the words of a favorite LDS hymn: "Do what is right, Let the consequence follow."

A good farmer plants, nourishes, weeds, and waters, then awaits the results, realizing he cannot control the ultimate fate of his fields any more than we can foresee our own destinies or the ultimate influence of our lives on others. No one can play God. Let us gain most of our satisfaction from our actions alone. Choosing how we act is within our control; the end results are not.

Gifts We Enjoy from the Service of Others and the Grace of God

"Even so, faith if it hath not works is dead."

(James 2:17)

"For by grace are ye saved through faith . . . not of works lest any man should boast." (Eph. 2:8, 9)

The above two scriptures seem to contradict each other. James believed that we are saved by faith and works, and Paul believed we are saved by the grace of Deity. Who is right? Both are right if they do not exclude the other. Some aspects of life are realized only by individual effort, and other elements come to us as pure gifts from the Creator and fellow beings. It is essential that we know which is which.

What are some of the things earned by individual effort? People learn to play the piano well by laborious hours of practice. Many give up because they are unwilling to persist. We become fluent in another language only through years of study. A builder erects a house through numerous learned sequential tasks. A farmer cannot expect a harvest unless he plows his field, plants his crops, and irrigates them.

The football player puts forth great effort to make the team and win the game. Few things are achieved in life without faith and works appropriate to the task.

What things come to us as gifts of grace, things that take no effort to obtain? Parley Christensen, a former BYU professor, once gave a Thanksgiving talk entitled "Unearned Goodness." He mentioned the many things you and I have received from those who have gone before us. Think of the pleasures and comforts of life—central heating, electric lights, telephone, radio, television, and the automobile.

Think of the gifts of medical science such as vaccinations protecting us from many diseases. Life expectancy has almost doubled in this century.

Our rich heritage of music—the works of Beethoven, Brahms, Chopin, Mozart, Verdi, Wagner, and countless other composers—have come to us through no effort of our own. Musical instruments that delight the ear—the piano, organ, percussion, string, and brass instruments—we have inherited through the genius of others.

Literature—the works of Shakespeare, Goethe, Keats, Emerson, Thoreau, Frost, and innumerable other authors—are ours for the asking. Religious classics, including the Bible, are not our creation but the product of great effort and insight by others.

The political freedom we enjoy in America and many countries of the world—government by law—is not of our own making. We owe this form of government to many men, including John Locke, Washington, Franklin, Madison, Jefferson, and the unknown heroes who gave their lives for freedom.

The greatest gift of all is the gift of life itself. I didn't create my own life. I owe it to the Creator and to my earthly parents. And oh how I cherish it—the capacity to see, hear, think, love, create, inspire, remember, share with others. And we have the promise of eternal life in a more blessed state.

Yes, life is a gift of God. We didn't earn it. We were incapable of creating it. But what we do with this gift is largely up to us. Will we cherish it, nourish it with good thoughts and deeds? Without the grace of Deity, we would not *be*. Without faith and works God's gift of life is wasted on us.

Some neighbors and I planted a huge garden one year on my lot. We grew a great variety of vegetables, kept them free of weeds, gave produce to widows, and boasted about *our* garden with pride. We forgot that we shared the garden with him who made the sunshine, the soil, the water, the seeds, and gave us the strength and intelligence to cultivate the land.

To know life, we must not only recognize God's grace toward us but also be gracious in our own living. We must learn that it is more blessed to give than to receive. Friendship, marriage, family life, and all human relations need to be seasoned with grace without which they have less value or meaning.

Too often, we make unconscious demands on life. We concentrate on our needs and unfulfilled desires and as a result often feel disappointed and frustrated. If we thought of life as a gift, we might not demand nearly as much from it. And if we lived more graciously, giving of ourselves more freely to the well-being of others, many of our personal concerns would disappear, and life would become easier for all.

The Indispensable Central Role of Love

There are a number of ways for an individual to identify with religion, to feel that he or she is a religious person. One may entertain beliefs in God, Christ (for a Christian), and personal salvation and feel religious through private prayer and worship. Or one may study scripture and the history of a religious movement and become a scriptorian or a lay theologian. Membership in a church, especially one where members accept callings and share rituals, prayers, and songs with co-believers, reinforces religious experience.

These ways of being religious are all legitimate and meaningful, but one thing is lacking. One essential component of religion received great emphasis in the teachings of the prophets of Israel—Moses and especially Amos, Hosea, Micah, Isaiah, and Jeremiah.

In the eighth century B.C. the Israelites living in the Northern Kingdom of Israel were quite prosperous and apparently content with their position as the chosen people of God. They expressed their religious faith by offering sacrifices, singing hymns, playing violas, saying prayers, and celebrating new moons and the Passover.

One day Amos, a shepherd from the hills of Judea, went to Bethel, a shrine city in the kingdom of Israel, and proceeded to speak to the people. He got their attention by declaring that the Lord was going to punish all the nations surrounding Israel for their sins. He even included punishment to the kingdom of Judah from whence he came (Judah and Israel were not on friendly terms). Then he turned on the Israelites:

> Hear this word that the Lord hath spoken against you, O children of Israel, against the whole family which I brought up from the land of Egypt, saying,
>
> You only have I known of all the families of the earth: therefore I will punish you for all your iniquities.
>
> Can two walk together, except they be agreed? Will a lion roar in the forest, when he hath no prey? . . .
>
> The lion hath roared, who will not fear? The Lord hath spoken, who can but prophesy? (Amos 3:1-3, 8)

The Lord roared, as it were, against his chosen people, Israel, through a lowly shepherd. Jehovah rejected Israel's traditional religious worship and practices.

> I hate, I despise your feast days, and I will not smell in your solemn assemblies.
>
> Though ye offer me burnt offerings and your meat offerings, I will not accept them: neither will I regard the peace offerings of your fat beasts.

> Take thou away from me the noise of thy songs; for I will not hear the melody of thy viols.
>
> But let judgment [justice] run down as waters, and righteousness as a mighty stream. (Amos 5:21-24)

Why did the Lord reject Israel's religious worship? Because in their daily lives they were selfish and dishonest and unmerciful towards the poor. The Lord would not have a people who were dishonest or unjust and who, while living in comfort, ignored the needs of widows and orphans.

Again the words of Amos:

> Woe to them that are at ease in Zion . . .
>
> That lie upon beds of ivory, and stretch themselves upon their couches, and eat the lambs out of the flock, and the calves out of the midst of the stall;
>
> That chant to the sound of the viol, and invent to themselves instruments of musick, like David;
>
> That drink wine in bowls, and anoint themselves with the chief ointments: but they are not grieved for the affliction of Joseph. (Amos 6:1, 3-6)

Amos, Micah, Isaiah, Moses, and Jeremiah make it clear that God is an ethical being, a person of integrity and mercy, and that no form of religious living is acceptable to him by people who are unjust and unmerciful. In other words, there can be no spirituality without social morality, a form of religion called ethical monotheism. God is one and ethical. Those who would worship him must be ethical in their dealings with their fellow human beings.

Isaiah, in his own delightful, colorful way, reinforced the teaching of Amos. His first chapter reveals the whole gamut of prophetic teaching.

> Hear, O heavens, and give ear, O earth: for the Lord hath spoken, I have nourished and brought up children, and they have rebelled against me.

The ox knoweth his owner, and the ass his master's crib: but Israel doth not know, my people doth not consider. (Isa. 1:2-3)

What an analogy! The dumb ox and the stupid ass know their master and where they are fed, but the Israelites do not understand their maker. They are no better than the people of Sodom and Gomorrah. Isaiah, speaking for the Lord, rejects the whole religious life of Israel. (See Isa. 1:11-14, 16.) The prophet Micah expresses this teaching most succinctly.

> Wherewith shall I come before the Lord, and bow myself before the high God? Shall I come before him with burnt offerings, with calves of a year old?
>
> Will the Lord be pleased with thousands of rams, or with ten thousands of rivers of oil? shall I give my firstborn for my transgression, the fruit of my body for the sin of my soul?
>
> He hath shewed thee, O man what is good; and what doth the Lord require of thee, but *to do justly, and to love mercy, and to walk humbly with thy God?* (Micah 6:6-8; emphasis added)

The distinctive emphasis of the Hebrew prophets maintains that morality—justice and mercy in human relations—must be present to make other forms of worship acceptable to God. Religion cannot be equated with ethics, but neither can it be void of morality.

We owe much to the Hebrew prophets for giving proper place to morality in the religious life. Their teaching of ethical-monotheism emphasizes one God of justice and mercy who can be truly worshipped and served only by humans who practice justice and mercy, repenting of their failures along the way.

Much of the Old Testament ritual rejected by the prophets, such as burnt offerings, has little meaning for us today. To sense the full impact of these prophetic teachings, we need to use present rituals. Wouldn't we be shocked if a prophet today speaking for God should say to the Saints:

> I hate your baptisms and sacrament service. I will not hear your prayers and songs anymore. Amen to your priesthood. Be honest in your dealings, be merciful to the poor and the afflicted, be understanding of the needs of others. Then my spirit will be with you and you will know me.

Amulek, a Book of Mormon prophet speaking about 74 B.C., was likewise prophetic in his teaching. In Alma 34 he encouraged his people to repent and to pray for their personal needs. Then he added:

> And now behold, my beloved brethren, I say unto you, do not suppose that this is all; for after ye have done all these things, if ye turn away the needy, and the naked, and visit not the sick and afflicted, and impart of your substance, if ye have, to those who stand in need—I say unto you, if ye

> do not any of these things, behold, your prayer is vain, and availeth you nothing, and ye are as hypocrites who do deny the faith.
>
> Therefore, if ye do not remember to be charitable, ye are as dross, which the refiners do cast out (it being of no worth) and is trodden under foot of men. (Alma 34:28–29)

Jesus, like the prophets before him, also laid great stress on moral relations among people. Unique to his ethical teaching was his great emphasis on love. A Pharisee, who was also a lawyer, asked Jesus:

> Master, which is the great commandment in the law?
>
> Jesus said unto him, Thou shalt love the Lord thy God with all thy heart, and with all thy soul, and with all thy mind.
>
> This is the first and great commandment.
>
> And the second is like unto it, Thou shalt love thy neighbour as thyself.
>
> On these two commandments hang all the law and the prophets. (Matt. 22:36-40)

Jesus did not originate these two commandments. Both appear in the law of Moses (Deut. 6:5 and Lev. 19:18), but Jesus added two significant additions. He made the second like unto the first, linking love of neighbor with love of God. Then he added that everything in the law and the prophets—in the accepted scripture of the day—hung or depended on love. Love formed the infrastructure of the gospel and of life—the central, most basic principle that should be part of every deliberation and action.

Throughout his life Jesus taught and exemplified the centrality of love. He was particularly concerned toward the end of his life that his disciples understand the role of love. He said:

> A new commandment I give unto you, That ye love one another; as I have loved you, that ye also love one another.
>
> By this shall all men know that ye are my disciples, if ye have love one to another. (John 13:34-35)

On judgment day Jesus will identify with the alienated of our society.

> When the Son of man shall come in his glory, and all the holy angels with him, then shall he sit upon the throne of his glory:
>
> And before him shall be gathered all nations: and he shall separate them from one another, as a shepherd divideth his sheep from the goats:
>
> And he shall set the sheep on his right hand, but the goats on the left.
>
> Then shall the King say unto them on his right hand, Come, ye blessed of my Father, inherit the kingdom prepared for you from the foundation of the world:
>
> For I was an hungered, and ye gave me meat: I was thirsty, and ye gave me drink: I was a stranger, and ye took me in:
>
> Naked, and ye clothed me: I was sick, and ye visited me: I was in prison, and ye came unto me.
>
> Then shall the righteous answer him, saying, Lord, when saw we thee an hungered, and fed thee? or thirsty, and gave thee drink?

> When saw we thee a stranger, and took thee in? or naked, and clothed thee?
>
> Or when saw we thee sick, or in prison, and came unto thee?
>
> And the King shall answer and say unto them, Verily I say unto you, Inasmuch as ye have done it unto one of the least of these my brethren, ye have done it unto me. (Matt. 25:31-40)

The apostle Paul, who made Jesus central to the religious life, grasped the place of love in the gospel of Jesus Christ. Word had come to Paul that his converts in Corinth were quarreling over who among them had the greater gifts. Some were especially pleased that they could speak in tongues (read 1 Cor. 12 and 14). Paul puts things in proper perspective in 1 Corinthians chapter 13. (The word *charity* in this text, translated from Greek, means Christian love.)

> Though I speak with the tongues of men and of angels, and have not charity, I am become as sounding brass, or a tinkling cymbal. And though I have the gift of prophecy, and understand all mysteries, and all knowledge; and though I have all faith, so that I could remove mountains, and have not charity, I am nothing. (1 Cor. 13:1–2)

A modern revelation, "And remember in all things the poor and the needy, the sick and the afflicted, for he that doeth not these things, the same is not my disciple" (D&C 52:40) reflects this same philosophy.

In the restoration of the gospel one would expect the heavy emphasis on theology and church organization, that is present. But there is also a great emphasis on the moral aspects of the gospel. A law of consecration was revealed to Joseph Smith which stressed equality and providing for widows and the poor. I called on an elderly widow one day to assess her circumstances and needs. She said her only family nearby was a granddaughter whom she hadn't seen for six months. I said, "You must get pretty lonely, don't you?"

She replied, "No, I don't. I have my God."

Paul as well as two great Book of Mormon prophets, Mormon and Moroni, joined Jesus in emphasizing the indispensable central role of love in life and in the gospel. If love is that important, we should do our best to understand its nature, how it can be lived, and how we can develop greater Christian love in our lives

Service: A Basic Value of the Religious Life

People who think of themselves as religious must decide how best to live their religion. There are many ways to be religious: going to church, worshipping publicly or privately, paying tithes and fast offerings, holding a position in the church, participating in ordinances such as baptism, confirmation, ordination.

We previously referred to the prophet Micah, who phrased the question nicely, "Wherewith should I come before the Lord and bow myself before the high God?" Then he answered his own question.

> Wherewith shall I come before him with burnt offerings, with calves of a year old?
>
> Will the Lord be pleased with thousands of rams or with ten thousands of rivers of oil? shall I give my first born for my transgression, the fruit of my body for the sin of my soul?
>
> He hath shewed thee, O man, what is good; and what doth the Lord require of thee, but to do

> justly, and to love mercy, and to walk humbly with thy God? (Micah 6:6–8)

Micah placed little value on rituals. Most important to him were religious-ethical principles applied to man's relationship to fellow humans and to God.

Justice, mercy, and humility are principles—basic ideas—that relate to an important area of life. Jesus lived and taught by principles. One Sabbath day in the synagogue, he saw a man with a withered hand. He healed the hand. This startled the Pharisees who witnessed it. They thought of religion in terms of specific dos and don'ts. The Mosaic Law forbade them to heal on the Sabbath. Jesus said in response, "I will ask you one thing; Is it lawful on the sabbath days to do good, or to do evil? to save life, or to destroy it?" (Luke 6:6–9). Jesus continued to think in terms of principles and their relationship to life.

Years ago I was invited to speak in a sacrament meeting by a former student who was a member of the bishopric of that ward. After the meeting, he invited me to his home.

Upon our arrival he turned on the TV—which was quite a new thing. We watched a movie starring Dorothy Gish, a flapper of the twenties. It was a silly show hardly in keeping with the spirit we had enjoyed at the sacrament meeting.

My host laughed and laughed. He was a devout Latter-day Saint who would never go to a movie on Sunday. But no one had laid down a rule against watching a Sunday show on television, so he was comfortable in doing it. People can live their religion either on the basis of rules or of principles.

The Sabbath has two basic purposes: to honor the Lord and to bless fellow human beings. Any activity that draws us nearer to God and brings healing and comfort to others is appropriate for the Sabbath. Living by these fundamentals gives us a sense of freedom and creativity in regard to the commandment to honor the Sabbath. These basic guides can keep us from inconsistencies and contradictions.

One Sunday morning during Sunday School, word came to the ward that our neighbor's furniture store was flooded with water threatening much damage. We gladly dismissed the Gospel Doctrine class, hurried to his store, and spent the Sabbath morning working—with a clear conscience—removing water.

We read that on one occasion Pharisees brought a woman to Jesus and said, "This woman is caught in adultery, in the very act. According to the law of Moses, she should be stoned. What sayest thou?" Even though he was opposed to adultery, Jesus answered in terms of principles rather than rules. He said to the Pharisees, "He who is without sin, let him cast the first stone." They walked away one by one. Jesus asked the woman, "Hath no man condemned thee?" She replied, "No man, Lord." Jesus said, "Neither do I condemn thee. Go thy way and sin no more" (see John 8:3–11).

One of the great things about Jesus as a teacher is that he laid down basic principles and often illustrated them unforgettably in parables such as the good Samaritan (mercy) and the prodigal son (forgiveness). The Beatitudes form a map of life in fundamental terms. They find application and meaning in a great variety of circumstances.

The value of teaching by principle can be illustrated by the Word of Wisdom. We usually stress the Word of Wisdom's admonition to avoid the use of alcohol, tobacco, tea, and coffee. This is important and valuable, but we can keep these rules and damage our health in other ways—by eating too much junk food, sugar, or salt, by working under stress, and by not exercising regularly.

I once guided a tour group of Latter-day Saints through countries of Europe. They were a fine group who lived their religion, at least the letter of the law. They didn't drink beer in Munich or coffee in Vienna. But some of them drank several cans of Coke every day.

The Word of Wisdom has no rule against drinking Coke. A person may drink as much as he pleases and still obtain a temple recommend.

But the Word of Wisdom revelation states that it is "given for a principle." That principle, I believe, is this: All things good for us, partake of in moderation and with thanksgiving. All things not good for us, have the wisdom to abstain from.

Of course many substances harmful to the body are not mentioned specifically, such as drugs or even caffeine. Living by the principle of the Word of Wisdom, we would eliminate items from our diet that would not promote good health and include in our diet those that do. And we would do a lot of positive things to enhance health—like exercising and getting enough sleep.

Living by rules can be restricting and lead to contradictions. Living by principles enables one to adjust to any circumstance with a feeling of integrity and creativity. Rules derive their meaning from principles. Principles derive their meaning and value from their contribution to life.

From life we derive principles, from principles, rules in descending importance but all related to each other.

LIFE

↓ ↑

PRINCIPLES

↓ ↑

RULES

Principles bring us into positive relationships with our fellow human beings. Integrity and love, for instance, I consider as the most basic principles that build rich human relationships *and* our relationship to Diety. The other principle that enables us to relate to God is faith. I don't need to exercise faith in integrity and love. I know from experience the value of these principles and the consequences of not living by them. But my relationship to God rests in part on faith. I have reasons to believe in God, but I have neither seen him nor heard his voice nor experienced him as directly as I have his teachings. Faith gives us adventure and excitement in our religious living. Someone has defined faith as reason grown courageous.

If there were no God, however, gospel principles would *still* give us the richest kind of life. Together with three other principles—to do justly and love mercy and walk humbly—integrity and love comprise the most significant elements in gospel living.

To do justly, love mercy, and walk humbly is part of integrity and love. Integrity includes justice and much more—persons of integrity display no pretense or guile. They profess values of their own choosing and live in harmony with them. Love includes mercy but other things as well. Persons who love their neighbors are tolerant, forgiving, helpful, and empathic. Integrity and love include all other virtues pertaining to our dealings with people.

In considering humility, as suggested by Micah's plea "to walk humbly with thy God," we should recognize our limited understanding of life compared with that of the greatest intelligence in the universe— who has encouraged us to ask, that we might receive, to seek, that we might find, and to knock, that the door to understanding might be opened unto us. We also need forgiveness of others and ourselves, which is Deity's right to give.

To be humble means also to live with gratitude. I'm so grateful for the experiences of mortality, for marriage and family life, countless friends, the bounties of nature, and the artistic creations of fellow beings. I'm glad for the uses of the mind: imagination, reflection, memory, and the ability to communicate with words.

To be grateful for such blessings is different from either the arrogance or the self-pity that might compare one's blessings with someone else's. Being grateful for life, for every day, is to be privately living the gospel with faith and conviction.

SECTION TWO

Making Critical Decisions: Advice to Youth

Choosing a Career

When Adam and Eve were driven out of the Garden of Eden, where life was easy, the curse or promise ringing in Adam's ears was "in the sweat of thy face shalt thou eat bread" (Gen. 3:19). Work has always been part of human life; however, rarely have individuals had as much freedom to freely *choose* their careers as we have today.

Such choices have always been constrained by options available in society at large and further restricted by family rank, social class, economic leverage, education, and traditions. In ancient worlds, including that of the Savior, captives were enslaved. In feudal society, the labor of whole families was subject to the demands of their lord. Even in modern times, vocational choice has been limited to family apprenticeships when education was available.

A young American lives in a country where public education costs little and where a wealth of career opportunities await. In taking advantage of these, few pleasures are so fulfilling as work that can make a contribution to other people and give one a sense of mastering a craft or skill. For generations young women's crafts lay largely within the home circle, and they were respected for their homemaking skills as much as men were respected for their ability to scythe a field of wheat. As more and more of a woman's tasks (such as weaving cloth, preserving food, and nursing the sick) shifted to professionals outside of the home, the respect and status accorded homemakers diminished.

Women of my generation made considerable sacrifices to be wives and mothers, performing that vital work with sensitivity and courage because they had the vision to see its importance even when others condemned it as limiting. But by and large, they had to choose that role because there were few viable ways to combine parenthood and careers. Men also, by and large, had to be full-time breadwinners and part-time parents.

I am delighted that this situation is changing. Now women of my granddaughters' generation can enjoy the satisfactions and challenges of making a contribution to the world outside the home as well as savoring the joys of wifehood and motherhood; I am equally delighted that men of my grandsons' generation can make a serious commitment to the mingled responsibilities and delights of fatherhood while also achieving in the careers they have chosen.

But perhaps we need to stress the word *choice*. How do we choose a career and prepare for it? The first step is to finish high school. About 20 percent of those in high school drop out before graduation. This is a tragic waste of ability and potential. Even though students may be impatient with the system or unhappy at the sheer effort required to achieve at the levels they would like, it is important to be patient and diligent. High school is an essential step.

The next step is to get specific training, either at a college or at a trade/technical school. To be broadly educated and work in a profession like medicine, engineering, dentistry, law, or education, a university education is basic. But there are many additional choices in the world of technical training. Secretarial work, plumbing, appliance repair, electrical work or electronics, food services, certain levels of nursing, and carpentry are only a few of the technical careers open through specialized training programs.

One might be drawn to the university because of the additional, though wrongfully placed, status sometimes accorded to college graduates. Although the broad general education that each university graduate receives is enriching, a diligent reader can do much in the way of self-education. Society needs many more workers with solidly-based vocations than it needs university professors, even though my own association with the university has been a source of great pleasure to me. The world needs auto mechanics who understand and enjoy the challenges of readjusting a machine for better functioning. I respect professionalism and craftsmanship whether I encounter it in a well-developed book, a beautifully constructed piece of furniture, or a smoothly organized dental office.

In addition to the enormous satisfactions of being able to do something well, there is enjoyment in the security that comes from having a marketable skill. People without training have only their labor to exchange for the necessities of life. They are the first laid off; and when they do have a job, they are paid a minimum wage. Being dependent on unemployment benefits, while a reassuring cushion for temporary setbacks, is debilitating and depressing.

Choosing a career is not an easy decision. Lucky are the students who know what they want to do while still in high school and can shape training, part-time jobs, and hobbies in that direction. But most will not know what they want as a vocation until they have had more experience in life. That is not bad. Hardly anyone keeps the same job or even works in the same field for an entire lifetime. Far more important than choosing a trade are two other things: (1) Learning how to learn so that, whenever it becomes necessary, we can change to fit new circumstances, and (2) Finding something that gives pleasure and interest.

From my association with students, I recall that most of them felt disturbed at the idea of changing majors; but it was really quite common for the average student to change majors two or three times. As part of the information age we live in, it is vital to obtain a solid background in computers, writing, and mathematics. These basic skills will serve as a solid base no matter what the eventual career.

I have already mentioned the opportunities available for women in education and careers. Let me stress that young women have the same need and responsibility to obtain education and training as young men. They have the same human hunger to express themselves creatively. They have a right to self-realization that comes with learning and growing intellectually and socially. They, too, should feel competent as part of the adult world. They desire as much out of careers as men do.

If you are a young woman, consult your desires, ambitions, and needs. Do not accept any limitations that someone may try to place on you, either directly or by innuendo, because they think a particular activity or goal is "not appropriate" for a woman. If you are a young man, associate with young women who want to be the best they can—not those who are passive and uninterested in engaging life fully.

These are the psychological reasons for women to be educated and trained. But there are economic reasons as well that must be faced realistically. A young woman might not marry. If she does, there is no guarantee that her marriage will be a permanent one. Fifty percent of American marriages end in divorce. Even if the marriage remains intact, the husband may lose his breadwinning capacity through shifts in the job market that leave him unemployed for short or long periods of time. He may become incapacitated or he may die.

Even if a marriage prospers, and the woman chooses to be a full-time homemaker, I would still urge her to get an education and training. Such a background will make her life more interesting. It will connect her with the broader community and give her new directions in which to continue growing. She will be a better wife, mother, church worker, and community member. She will feel more secure and confident, knowing she can earn a living if she needs or wishes to do so.

Having training, even if you choose not to use it immediately, gives you many more options in the future. Some women, whether married or single, work full time for a variety of reasons, including their desire to feel creative and productive. Others work part time, to give more time to home responsibilities or personal needs. Whatever your situation, preparation increases your options.

Considerations for Choosing a Mate

Every Sunday morning I enjoy looking at the pictures of bridal couples in the newspaper, noting their smiles as they anticipate the happiness awaiting them in marriage. Their optimism is understandable because they are in love, and marriage in our society is supposed to lead to deeper and more abiding love. Marriage can fulfil that very basic need of every human being to be accepted, cherished, and loved. We are social as well as individual by nature.

Before she died at the age of eighty-eight, my wife and I were married for over sixty-five years. It was a wonderful relationship, a delightful partnership, a happy conjunction of two different people with strengths, resources, and weaknesses of their own who became better by their association. I look at those happy faces with the secret hope that, fifty years from now, each couple will know the happiness that Merle and I experienced.

Despite the great potential for joy in marriage, the hard reality is that about half of American marriages end in divorce. Of those that endure, many partners merely tolerate each other. What leads to so many failures and so much disappointment?

Could it be that we are not well prepared to cope with the challenges of marriage? Even the best of marriages will entertain occasional differences between husbands and wives. Whether the differences are small and inconsequential or more serious, they call for negotiation and problem solving skills.

Any discussion of coping must include separate consideration of this all-important relationship. Why does a good marriage require so much effort to be successful? Is there a way to help people already married to avoid difficulties as well as to prepare those anticipating marriage so that they will have less coping to do?

Could a major reason for so many failures lie in the fact that the circumstances under which we decide to marry often have little resemblance to the nature of marriage itself? Many of us marry primarily because we are romantically attracted to each other, because we are in love. Although being in love is one good reason to marry, by itself it is not an adequate basis for a healthy marriage. Romantic attraction is all we need to make dating pleasant and to instill faith in a more lasting bond between a couple. But marriage extends far beyond a romantic relationship. Affection plays a big role in marriage, even larger than in courtship days, but in a much broader context.

While dating, we share and enjoy each other's affections and dreams; then we separate and go our own ways to school, work, home life with parents and siblings, or to friends of our own sex. But in marriage, affection must blend with living habits, attitudes, work, differences of opinion, illness, pregnancy, financial concerns, and much more.

I recall a couple who came to me for help when I was their bishop. She was pregnant and suffering from nausea, but her husband flatly refused to do the cooking and dishes. His father had forced him to do these chores as a boy, and he had sworn he would never do them again when he left home. His wife naturally felt that his attitude was unreasonable and unfair. Fortunately, it was a relatively simple matter to convince him that leaving home had ended his battle with his parents. He had no need to carry the same fight into his own home.

Marriage involves a total relationship of two unique personalities in an ever-changing situation. Therein lies both its value and its frustration. A mature, married love is very different from the love of courtship. Within marriage, romance, friendship, and Christian love (or love of neighbor) should blend into one. Romantic love, while ecstatic, is based on our physical natures and by itself can become fickle and unstable. Friendship is creative togetherness, a sharing of common interests and values, a sheer delight in each other's company, a mysterious kind of kinship where spirit meets spirit. Friendship gives substance to romantic love, adding, among other things, an intellectual dimension. Christian love is a genuine interest in the well-being of the other person. It is kind, considerate, thoughtful, forgiving, tender, and selfless, whereas romantic love tends to be self-seeking and demanding. The ideal love in marriage consists of romance enriched by friendship and refined by Christian love.

Marriages have not always been based on love. In ancient India and China, for example, parents often arranged marriages for their children on the basis of economic and social compatibility. Ironically, those marriages may have proven more successful than today's marriages based on romance. However, I much prefer the modern way of choosing our own mates, though I wish that we could be more realistic, choosing with our heads as well as our hearts. To that end, let me offer a few suggestions.

Let us first examine the nature of marriage. I find three basic relationships in marriage: a financial and working partnership, an everyday total human association, and an affectionate, loving relationship. Never separate, isolated aspects of marriage, these are experienced together and influence each other.

A FINANCIAL AND WORKING PARTNERSHIP

We live in a capitalist economy. Gone are the pioneer days when a couple could homestead free land, build a log house, raise food, spin their own clothing, and thus survive by the labor of their hands. Modern living requires cash to rent or buy a home, pay for utilities, insurance, a car and gas, and health care. This means that the husband or wife or both need a job.

Couples face the inevitable problem of deciding how to spend the money they earn. They bring different attitudes and practices to money matters, coming from households with inevitable differences in their attitudes toward money. One may be frugal, the other careless; one tight, the other generous.

The best way for a couple to reach an understanding in financial matters is to budget together their income and expenditures and stick to their plan. Budgeting is an education in economic values. A couple can divide the responsibility of managing the budget. To retain a measure of privacy, each can have a personal monthly fund with no questions asked about how it is spent.

Most young couples start life on a shoestring, and many couples in later years still find themselves struggling to make ends meet, for expenses have risen along with increased earning power. My salary was never excessive throughout our married life; and it has, fortunately, been a source of great satisfaction to both of us to be able to manage our limited resources successfully.

Let me offer a few suggestions to help any couple live on a tight budget. Try to minimize the use of charge accounts and credit cards. They encourage spending and make expenditures difficult to keep track of. Pay as you go whenever possible. Distinguish between needs and wants. The latter are innumerable, the former much more limited. Cultivate things which do not depend on money or much of it: reading, conversing, walking, visiting, listening to good music, working at inexpensive hobbies. I have always believed fervently in these words of the Savior: "Lay up for yourselves treasures in heaven, where neither moth nor rust doth corrupt, and where thieves do not break through nor steal" (Matt. 6:20).

As a corollary of financial responsibility in marriage, I also urge every couple to accept and rejoice in the fact that marriage is a working partnership. It takes much cooperative labor to maintain a yard and a house or an apartment.

For the sake of efficiency and to give both husband and wife some sense of freedom, a division of labor is desirable. But gone are the days when the wife took care of housework and child care. The husband should share in this labor, all the more so if his wife is also employed outside of the home. When either is ill or especially burdened, the other should pitch in and share the workload. I would feel truly helpless and limited in my ability to serve others if I could not prepare a meal for my wife when she is ill or for a neighbor in need.

AN EVERYDAY, HUMAN ASSOCIATION

A second aspect of marriage is its everyday human association. It is impossible to mask your character and personality in the everyday, multifaceted life of marriage. Being together has its good side; there is always someone there who cares, who can be counted on come what may. On the other hand, togetherness brings an awareness of habits, attitudes, and mannerisms that may be difficult to endure day after day. Living together through the years, including retirement, is a challenge for any couple. What can we do to maximize the positive aspects of this intimate daily relationship?

The first thing is to respect the individuality of your spouse. No two individuals think and feel alike. We are all unique, having come from different upbringings and being male and female. We may be seriously tempted to make our partners over in our own image, but the message of any such attempt is: "You are unacceptable to me. I don't like you the way you are." A marriage in which such an attitude prevails is headed for disaster.

In our traditionally male-dominated society, some husbands seek to be in full command. They expect their wives to obey them, to follow their lead as patriarch of the family. Whatever differences exist between men and women—and I believe there are some important ones—autonomy or control over one's life is a basic human need. Any attempt to reduce the freedom or dominate the agency of another is just as bad within marriage as it is in other settings. Marriage is a partnership. That means that both man and woman must contribute equally, though perhaps in different ways, and benefit equally. All too often, a patriarchal orientation means the woman is contributing and the man is benefiting. I see equal possibilities for imbalance in the attitudes of some feminists as well. Neither extreme is good for full human development.

Marriage partners must also respect their own individuality. Marriage is not a crutch. We cannot depend upon our spouses to bring us happiness. That can come only through our own thinking, feeling, serving, and learning. A female university student confided to me in my office one day, "If only I were married, I'd be happy." Pity the poor fellow she marries, I thought. No human being can be fully responsible for the happiness of another.

One of the best ways to contribute to others' happiness is to assist them in satisfying what I consider their basic psychological needs:

1. To be accepted and loved by other human beings.
2. To be productive and creative, thus justifying their existence.
3. To feel their own worth.
4. To find meaning and purpose in living.

A spouse can do more than anyone else to help a marriage partner satisfy those needs. Couples can love and accept each other for what they are, as they are. They can encourage and praise each other in their efforts to be creative and productive. I have discussed the importance of accepting ourselves as we are (Chapter 3) and in cultivating integrity by behaving in ways that reflect our individual values (Chapter 3 and 8). These concepts are the true foundation of self-esteem and the way of liberating ourselves from misguided attempts to improve our self-esteem by methods that basically do not work. However, in addition to our own integrity and achievement, we must also acknowledge the important effects on our self-esteem of the love, respect, and praise of the significant other people in our lives. Married couples should never belittle or demean each other. They should offer criticism infrequently, in private, and only in a context of love.

It is much more effective to strengthen each other's good qualities than to single out what we consider limitations. A master key to a couple's successful everyday relationship is the ability to communicate with a minimum of offense and a maximum of tolerance seasoned by plenty of good humor.

A BOND OF AFFECTION

Lovemaking in marriage is more than physical, more than instinctive. It is an expression of a total relationship. A student in one of my marriage classes at the Institute once asked: "What is the art of making love in marriage?" One answer came from a happily married woman in the class who said: "The art of making love in marriage is a kind word."

We have mentioned three kinds of love between a man and a woman: romance, friendship, and Christian love of neighbor. Romantic love is greatly enriched by the creative togetherness of friendship, by having values and interests in common, and by delighting in each other's company. Romantic love is refined by unselfishness, kindness, and thinking of the other person's well-being and happiness. Great lovers in marriage are those individuals who bring the deepest friendship and finest Christian consideration to their affection.

Love is mutual. This may seem obvious, but it means that neither partner in a relationship can be truly happy unless both are. Selfishness in love is self-defeating as well as aggravating to a spouse.

Lovemaking is an art—not a contrived art, but one born of consideration for the feelings of a spouse. Men and women differ in their emotional responses to affection. The husband may be impatient in his desire for gratification while his wife may need more time to find sexual fulfillment. She wishes to be desired as a total human being, not as a sex object.

Years of observation and counseling have convinced me that it is terribly important—absolutely essential—for a couple to be true to each other and to avoid any other romantic relations. Infidelity destroys the integrity of the violator and the love and trust between the couple. Although such trust can be rebuilt, it is extremely difficult to do so. Integrity and love are the primary principles of the moral life, and all other ethical virtues are merely expressions of them.

Marriage affords the opportunity to experience the richest kind of love possible between human beings—a blend of romantic feeling, creative friendship, and genuine concern for the well-being of another person. Though the meaning of these kinds of love will change in any given marriage, the possibility of knowing the fullest meaning of love is always present.

A SUCCESSFUL APPROACH TO MARRIAGE

If our discussion to this point helps us better understand marriage, then how can we approach that union in a way consistent with its real character? Since romantic love is blind, it needs to be preceded by an assessment of other relationships in marriage. A couple should be assured of each other's good character and friendship before giving way to romantic feeling. How do we do this?

Avoid steady dating before you have tested a partner's character and friendship. Steady dating builds an obligation and easily turns into an affectionate relationship. I recommend going out with two or three people over the same period of time. This helps keep relationships on a friendship basis.

Once a student invited my wife and me to ride to a college party with her and her escort. I have never ridden before or since with anyone as discourteous, loquacious, or inconsiderate as my friend's escort. A couple of days later, she remarked candidly, "I think the way he drives is the way he is. I hope I never see him again."

One of my colleagues on campus recommended that people observe potential friends in the classroom and other settings and get to know what kind of reputation they have before dating them. I have told my students or other people who have asked for advice, "Never marry anyone you haven't served on a committee with. Such activity reveals the other person's capacity for dependability, creativity, teamwork, leadership, flexibility, humor, and much else."

Before student wards and stakes were organized at the University of Utah, our Institute of Religion sponsored a Sunday School. In keeping with church tradition, the superintendency consisted of three young men. The organist and chorister also happened to be men. The only woman officer was our secretary. Observing the one-sidedness of our officers' corps, we decided to call five young women to serve on a committee to help us program special Sunday services such as Christmas, Easter, and Mother's Day, to serve as an enlistment committee, and to advise us on the Sunday School program in general. Two happy marriages developed out of this ongoing association.

Group activities and associations—small firesides, discussions following concerts, lectures, or church meetings—reveal interests and mental qualities. So does person-to-person conversation, especially when stimulated by a substantive topic. Years ago I read a study reporting that marriages of college students had a higher success rate than those of non-students of the same age, presumably because the college experience gave people intellectual interests to share.

PREPARING FOR MARRIAGE

A student in a marriage class I taught said, "Happiness in marriage doesn't depend as much on finding the right person as it does on being the right person." Even though this point of view has been used unfairly against women, making them accommodate more than their share and even keeping them in abusive situations, I heartily agree, since it applies to a man as much as to a woman. Our attitude is by far the most important ingredient in the mixture. And both partners need to agree on that. Perhaps we can conclude this discussion with a few questions for those contemplating marriage:

1. Are you happy without marriage, based on your own resources?
2. Are you prepared to earn a living or are you moving successfully in that direction? (This applies to both men and women.)
3. Do you have a good measure of integrity? Are you honest? Do you have moral convictions you live up to?
4. Do you love your neighbor? Do you have compassion and tolerance for people different from you?
5. Do you have interests—intellectual, cultural, social, religious—that will contribute to a rich friendship?

6. Do you like children and enjoy their company?

7. Do you have opportunities to associate with groups of people near your age in interesting ways?

I hope that fifty years from now you, too, can celebrate the richly satisfying, multifaceted relationship that constitutes true marriage.

What about Sex?

THREE KINDS OF LOVE

Couples can experience three kinds of love: romantic love, friendship love, and Christian love. Romantic love is ecstatic and can be experienced very rapidly. It is based in good measure on physical attraction and natural reactions. It is very exciting and all-consuming. When in love, you become very conscious that you are!

Friendship usually develops over time. It has a broader base. It involves minds as well as bodies. Friends have common interests, are loyal to each other, and trust each other with who they are and how they feel. Someone has defined friendship as "creative togetherness."

Christian love is the most selfless and unselfish kind of love. The Apostle Paul expresses the nature of Christian love most beautifully in 1 Corinthians:

> Though I speak with the tongues of men and of angels, and have not charity [love], I am become as sounding brass, or a tinkling cymbal.
>
> And though I have the gift of prophecy, and understand all mysteries, and all knowledge; and though I have all faith, so that I could remove mountains, and have not charity, I am nothing.

> And though I bestow all my goods to feed the poor, and though I give my body to be burned, and have not charity, it profiteth me nothing.
>
> Charity [Love] suffereth long, and is kind; charity envieth not; charity vaunteth not itself, is not puffed up,
>
> Doth not behave itself unseemly, seeketh not her own, is not easily provoked, thinketh no evil;
>
> Rejoiceth not in iniquity, but rejoiceth in the truth;
>
> Beareth all things, believeth all things, hopeth all things, endureth all things.
>
> Charity [Love] never faileth. (13:1-8)

Romantic love is sufficient for dating, but it is not an adequate basis for love in marriage. Love in marriage needs all three kinds of love. Romantic love is too unstable and fickle to be a solid basis for married love. That about half of the marriages in America end in divorce occurs probably in good part because they originate in romantic love. Romantic love doesn't have the depth or breadth to sustain a couple in the intimate and complex life of marriage.

These three types of love need to be cultivated in the right order. Friendship and ethical character should be developed first and romantic love, with its sexual implications, last. People who begin their relationship with romantic attraction and do not make a conscious effort to develop Christian love and friendship simultaneously run into a number of problems.

To preserve the intimacies of sex for marriage, I suggest, as a concerned and grandfatherly friend, that you make a firm commitment to yourself not to get involved in sexual intimacy until married. It might help to get a friend or two with similar standards to make the commitment with you. You should keep in mind the nonromantic consequences of too-early sexual intimacy and review them from time to time. They have a way of bringing a fuzzy romantic issue into sharp focus.

DATING

More and more I observe the healthy pattern of young people going in groups more than dating. Boys and girls in high school and college often gather at an event rather than go with one particular date. Or if they do date, they meet others to work on physical fitness or outdoor recreation or go to a movie or church activity with the group. This can afford a look at and opportunity to talk with many who share their interests and experience without moving quickly into the intimacy and sometimes pressure of being alone with one person.

Certainly I can understand the romantic impulse. I fell in love and married my wife, Merle, without dating anyone else. But after decades of observing human behavior, I realize that the success of a marriage like that may be pure luck.

For each of us, our response to romantic love is different. But give yourself a chance to meet as many others as you can. Chemistry we can't control: experience we can. Broaden your base. See another person in as many different circumstances as possible, especially when involved in a project or cause that will show how they operate outside of themselves.

There is no occupation like marriage. And unfortunately, there are not many courses in how to make a good one. Intimacy in marriage is important; but satisfying physical intimacy is closely linked with a satisfying relationship in general. To assess your possibilities as a likely candidate for a good marriage, here are some questions to ask yourself:

How able am I to organize? Can I forget myself even as I bring my best to what needs me? Can I cooperate? Or must I have my way? How dedicated am I to what needs me? How creative? Do I finish a job? Am I now and am I becoming more competent? Do I need to get credit? Or can I be more interested in what might work?

Can I compromise, work with others? Am I moody? Do I try to control others by my moods? Can I laugh? At myself? What might be a wretched outcome to well-intended effort? Am I appreciative? Do I show it? Am I able to express my feelings of affection, both verbally and physically?

Get acquainted not only with your own qualities that affect satisfaction when relating with another person but also with those of your possible marriage partner. Learn what to expect. Discuss how each of you feel about: religion, a family, children—when and how many you would want; the work you hope to do; people, travel, where to live; whether you would want to build a home, friends, learning; TV, music, entertainment, books; how you spend time when you have it to spare.

Ask: what are your parents like? What do you want to perpetuate of them? What do you believe in? What do you reverence? Who are your best friends? Why? What makes you angry? Sad? Happy? Grateful? How do you resolve conflict? How important is physical activity? Mental? Spiritual? How do you handle money? What are your priorities for spending? Is saving important? How is your health? How do you handle being sick?

After answering these questions for yourself and hearing and evaluating the answers of your would-be-partner, ask yourself if you are ready in indulge in sex that might rush you into a less than desirable relationship.

Not many of my generation, or probably the next, took the opportunity to ask such questions of each other before marriage. That my own marriage turned out well was a combination of luck, commitment, work, and willingness to make adjustments. I wonder about how our "luck" would have panned out had we been obliged or compelled by sexual as well as romantic complications?

According to recent studies, over 50 percent of young people have intimate sex relations while still in junior or senior high school. These statistics are not surprising, but they are alarming. Although my generation is in no position to point fingers at yours, this situation merits the concern that it arouses among parents, teachers, church leaders, and thoughtful young people themselves. If I may assume the role of a grandfather and be as candid as I would be with my own grandchildren, I would like to offer some of the most practical reasons why I think saving sex for marriage makes sense.

I understand some of the reasons for sexual experimentation. Television programs, movies, and much literature focuses on the sexual aspects of human relationships virtually to the exclusion of all other considerations. Pornography and sexually explicit material are much more easily available now than they used to be. Sexual development far precedes social, economic, emotional, and intellectual maturity. Adolescence is a time when people want to seek adventure, new experiences, and freedom from external constraints. Often these experiments take a sexual form. Often, if school lacks intellectual excitement, or if sports, hobbies, and service fail to attract a restless teen's attention, sex seems the least boring of alternative activities.

Sex is an important part of life, and I say that as someone who was happily married for almost seventy years. Sex can be either a joyful, life-fulfilling source of much happiness or the cause of much grief.

ADVICE TO MY GRANDCHILDREN

Young people should be especially concerned about sex outside of marriage because of the risk of pregnancy. If we were to make a decision diagram of the kinds of physical complications involved in unwed pregnancy—without consideration of social, emotional, and spiritual difficulties—it rapidly assumes a complex shape.

---

[1] Although the success level of some forms of contraception is much higher than others, no form is completely certain. Many married women using a prescribed contraceptive under the guidance of a physician have been surprised to find themselves pregnant. The only way to be sure you will not get pregnant is sterilization or abstinence.

Should we have sex?

No. In this case, pregnancy is not a problem.

Yes. This decision leads immediately to another question.

Should we use contraceptives?[1]

Yes. This decision leads to other questions.

What kind?

How do we choose?

How do we get them?

How do we use them?

How effective are they?

What if our folks find out?

No. This decision can lead to much emotional turmoil.

What if we get pregnant?

Should she get an abortion? If yes, what about:

the father's feelings?

the teachings of my church?

our parents' reactions?

my own emotional reactions?

Should we have the baby? If yes, then:

Can we get married? If yes:

what about money? a house? work? school?

Can we keep the baby?

Should we give it up for adoption?

Will my family help?

What about my church standing?

Each one of these questions branches off into other questions involving social, educational, personal, spiritual, familial, and economic consequences that are too snarled to put on a page. But if the answer to the question "Should we have sex?" is "No," then none of these other questions or consequences will follow.

There are other practical risks separate from the teachings of the Church, the spiritual consequences of breaking the law of chastity, or the emotional trauma of a sexual relationship outside of marriage.

For example, serious diseases are spread through sexual intercourse. Two of these—syphilis and gonorrhea—have been with us for centuries. Some of these diseases, like AIDS, have deadly consequences. Thus far, there is no sure way to prevent the sexual transmission of AIDS except by not engaging in sexual intercourse or by engaging in sexual intercourse only with a partner free of the HIV virus (which is difficult or impossible to determine without medical tests). Using a high-quality condom lowers the risk, but risk cannot be eliminated. This disease is, so far as we know, always progressive and always fatal.

I have not mentioned the emotional consequences of being sexually involved for both young men and young women. Nor have I mentioned the serious spiritual consequences of sexual activity outside of marriage. Often these arguments are not persuasive for young people. But certainly they reinforce the very compelling practical reasons for avoiding sex outside of marriage.

So if you were my grandchildren, I would ask you to set considerations of love and physical attraction to one side and consider these issues as tough-mindedly and objectively as possible. Having sex outside of marriage can cause problems of major proportions. It is a wise and mature decision to avoid unnecessary problems. Life will give you enough difficulties without seeking any out.

LOVE IN MARRIAGE

There is a difference between romance on a date and romantic love in marriage. In dating, you share an evening or an event. Even if romantic feelings are involved, you then separate and go your own ways to work or study after the evening is over. In contrast, when married, you live together as two total personalities in a total situation, bringing your whole relationship to your lovemaking in marriage.

Love in marriage is an expression of your total personality. Great lovers in marriage are those who have the deepest friendships and the finest Christian attitudes. Love in marriage is much more than a physical and physiological expression of erotic interest. One of the by-products of a good marriage can be freeing each partner to be his or her best self, to realize the full measure of that person's creation. It can mean support and closeness whether one works outside the home and the other is usually in the home or whether they both need to be gone for their daily work.

When I think of great married lovers, T. Edgar Lyon and Hermana Lyon always come to mind. Ed was my colleague at the Institute of Religion adjacent to the University of Utah for many years. I valued him greatly for his communications skills, his patience, his optimistic outlook, and his genuine concern for each individual he met. Even without knowing his wife, I could have predicted that Ed would be a wonderful marriage partner because of these skills.

But it was also my privilege to know Hermana. She and my wife, Merle, were close friends, and over the years we saw how Hermana and Ed's strong, loving companionship formed the foundation for the strengths they shared with others in many areas of their personal and professional lives. Ed's first instinct on getting an idea or learning a piece of news was to share it with Hermana, and hers was the same. Sometimes four or five phone calls a day passed between them. He was always anxious to go home at night after the day's work was done.

No one could have been more supportive of the long hours Ed spent in the service of students than Hermana (unless it was Merle's support of me), but she always anticipated his return with great joy. They were true sweethearts. They rejoiced in each other's presence, were proud of each other's accomplishments, were completely loyal to each other, and worked together as partners in all that they did. Faith and commitment were the foundation and walls of their house, but their romantic love for each other gilded the cornices, polished the furniture, and perfumed the air.

And I must pay tribute to my own companion of almost seventy years. I have never stopped marveling at the miracle that I, a young man with little wisdom, still had the incredible blessing of finding Merle and falling in love with her so securely over a long period of talking and working together that I knew, even before I left for my mission, that I wanted to be married to her forever. It says a great deal for her own faith, courage, and strength of love that she was willing to marry me under those circumstances and see me leave on my mission after our brief honeymoon, write to me faithfully while I was gone, and then join me in Europe, far from her family and mine, where we stayed three years while I completed a doctoral degree.

It would be hard to think of any operatic lovers who were more intensely (although I hope less flamboyantly) in love than we were. But our romantic love, intense though it was, was only part of our relationship. Our temple sealing, our intellectual interests, our commitment to church service, and our appreciation of art and culture were also important parts of our relationship. It was the totality of this relationship that gave us hope and comfort during one of the darkest seasons of our lives, when our first daughter was born, then died at the age of six months.

I don't think romantic love could survive such a blow, if it were the dominant element in a relationship. But because our romantic love was part of our total relationship, our feelings for each other became part of the gradual healing of our grief so that we could rejoice in a continued relationship and in the births of the children who followed.

Would we have felt such strong love for each other had we not saved the crowning intimacies of sex for our marriage? I suspect not.

FIDELITY IN MARRIAGE

It is equally important for couples to be true to each other. When you marry, you promise to cherish, honor, and love each other. If you marry in a temple, you do so with the faith that your commitment will last beyond death into eternity. One of the most beautiful aspects of marriage is being able to feel that you are the most highly regarded person in your spouse's eyes, the recipient of his or her full and special love.

All too frequently that trust is violated because the wife or husband becomes sexually involved with another person. Although it is a problem that neither men nor women have a monopoly on, I have counseled more often with adulterous husbands.

Frequently, such men have expressed feelings of shock and surprise because they had no intention of committing adultery. Little things led to bigger things, and unwise attitudes led to unwise actions. In contrast, I have also known men who maintained a mistress in another town, apparently without any remorse when they thought of their wives and children.

If you, either through purposeful action or by "accident," break your marriage vows of fidelity, how does it affect you? You have promised to be true to your spouse. If you have an affair and keep it a secret, you are living a lie. You are pretending to be what you are not. If you confess the affair, you must deal with the excruciating agony of guilt and shame, your spouse's loss of trust in you, and the possible destruction of your marriage.

How does your infidelity affect your spouse? His or her precious status of being uniquely loved is shattered. If you are not repentant or if your spouse is not forgiving, you face the pain and life-wrenching consequences of a divorce.

If there are children, how are they affected? Children thrive best in a home where husband and wife love, trust, and enjoy each other.

The two most basic ethical principles, which embrace all others, are integrity and love of neighbor. Infidelity violates them both. It also violates your relationship with God by breaking one of the ten commandments.

THE BEST SEX

Sex relations between husband and wife are sanctioned by Deity. The Lord said:

> Therefore shall a man leave his father and his mother, and shall cleave unto his wife: and they shall be one flesh. (Gen. 2:24)

Sexual relations between a man and a woman are not evil or good as such. They can be either depending on their nature. Sexual intercourse out of wedlock is not good because a couple is not in a position to love each other with their whole souls, nor are they prepared to receive offspring and build a family.

If you were my grandson, if you were my granddaughter, this is what I would wish for you: the best kind of sex because it is the best kind of love. Intimate sexual love is good for married couples because they have pledged their complete and lasting love to one another and have set about to prove it by living together in a loyal and trusting companionship. Marriage is a prize worth working and waiting for. Your most basic psychological need is to be accepted and loved by another human being. Sexual love—backed by a rich friendship and fine character—satisfies that need in a special and delightful way.

SECTION THREE

Ways of coping with life's challenges

Facing Adversity Courageously

Hugh Walpole, a prominent Victorian novelist, said, "It isn't life that matters but the faith we bring to it." What happens in life does matter. We should use our best judgment, available knowledge, and self-control to prevent and avoid human suffering and failure. We should not be complacent about evils and difficulties which we could avoid or eliminate through intelligent action. At best, life is rugged enough without our encouraging or condoning its tragedies.

But even if we do our level best to prevent trouble, it is very likely to happen along the way. We haven't learned, and probably never will, how to prevent earthquakes, volcanoes, hurricanes, floods, or droughts. These strike anywhere with seemingly no regard for the guilt or innocence of the human beings affected by them. "[The Lord] maketh his sun to rise on the evil and on the good, and sendeth rain on the just and on the unjust," the Savior reminded his listeners (Matt. 5:45). He counseled us to be like the wise man who built his house on the rock, not like the foolish man who built his house on the sand, because certainly the time would come when "the rain descended, and the floods came, and the winds blew, and beat upon" both houses (Matt. 7:27).

Living such gospel principles as integrity, love, faith, and humility will spare us much mental and spiritual anguish and the torments of feeling that life is meaningless; but it will not guarantee us freedom from natural disasters and afflictions. Cancer and multiple sclerosis strike sinner and saint alike. Living the Word of Wisdom will enable us to avoid drug addiction, alcoholism, and other ills. But our knowledge of medicine and therapy is too limited to spare us all grief and suffering from physical ailments.

In the end, sooner or later, nature gets the upper hand, from a mortal perspective. Old age relentlessly claims its place in the life cycle. And suffering and death come to one and all.

We "live, and move, and have our being" in each other as well as in nature and in the providence of Deity (Acts 17:28). We are enormously blessed by the contributions of our fellow human beings, by our social heritage. The comforts of life, freedom from many diseases, beautiful music, government by law, and the wisdom of ages past have come to us freely. On the other hand, we also suffer from acts of terrorism, drunken drivers, murder, rape, robbery, dishonesty, and deceit. We live uneasily under the threat of nuclear war, domestic violence, and a flood of illegal drugs.

What I am saying is that life is rich in both good and evil, in beauty and ugliness, in hope and despair. It is a proving ground, a test of our human spiritual strength. With Nephi, we will all find opposition in all things (2 Ne. 2). The big question remains: How do we cope with this mixture of good and evil, joy and sorrow, life and death?

Come what may, we can choose to face up to whatever occurs with courage and a life-affirming hope. I met a man in his late thirties. He was a big, strong policeman until he was struck with multiple sclerosis. I watched him deteriorate quickly, moving into a wheelchair and then to his bed, but he maintained perspective. One day, while conversing with him, he said jokingly, with not a trace of bitterness, "Doc, if it weren't for bad luck, I wouldn't have any luck at all." What a healthy, cheerful attitude! Instead of sinking into misery and hopelessness, he tried to make the best of a dismal situation.

Recently I called on a woman who has been bedfast for decades. She was all smiles as she counted her blessings and recited God's goodness to her, which has taught her the real values of life, such as "the kingdom of God is within you" (Luke 17:21). Sometimes the hardest experiences of life become our best teachers and the molders of our finest spiritual qualities. They do not leave us unaffected. Suffering either hardens us, leading to cynicism, or refines us, making us more patient. More important than what happens to us is our response to it.

A woman lost her only daughter and son-in-law and two of her beloved grandchildren in a plane crash. The family was en route to a ski vacation in Vermont. The son-in-law was an experienced pilot and flight instructor, and the twin-engine aircraft was fully equipped. But they never arrived at their destination. For eighty-seven days, the Civil Air Patrol and other volunteers searched for the victims.

Each conversation they had with the grieving family was a sweet experience, for they never failed to express appreciation and for the rescue efforts This gratitude did not lessen the loss, but it did mitigate the bitterness that could have afflicted the family. Thankfulness made them open to the support of others, enabling them to receive the love they needed at a difficult time. Nurturing their appreciation for the efforts and concern of others helped the family withstand the unbearable with grace and dignity.

In 1839 Joseph Smith and several companions spent months in Liberty Jail under deplorable conditions. While there, the Prophet received three remarkable revelations that became Sections 121-123 in the Doctrine and Covenants. The Lord comforted him by reassuring him that

> if the heavens gather blackness, and all the elements combine to hedge up the way; and above all, if the very jaws of hell shall gape open the mouth wide after thee, know thou, my son, that all these things shall give thee experience, and shall be for thy good.
>
> The Son of Man hath descended below them all. Art thou greater than he? (D&C 122:7-8)

I repeat, I am not glorifying suffering. It is not always of value. We cannot always control what happens to us, but we can control our responses to misfortune. When we endure hardship with a life-affirming attitude, we turn suffering into strength.

Gaining Control of Our Lives

Animals seem to act on instinct. Human beings, on the other hand, are self-conscious. We not only act and react, but we seem compelled by our nature to evaluate our actions. So we enjoy the pleasure of achievement, the stimulation of idealizing our interests and efforts, and we experience the disappointments and even the pains that accompany failure and wrongdoing. Self-consciousness is both our glory and our burden.

One of our heaviest burdens is sin—choosing to act contrary to what we believe is right. The mind functions best when it is unified, when we live in harmony with what we believe is right. When we fail to measure up to our self-imposed standards, we experience regret, sometimes even shame and guilt.

The question confronts us: How do we cope with a present weakness, failure, or sin? I will later discuss how we can change the past and be forgiven. In this essay our purpose is to deal with problems in the present. How do we overcome our weaknesses, our failures, our sins?

In many discussions I hear Satan blamed for the evil in our lives. He is described as the great tempter, the father of lies, the enemy of righteousness. The New Testament, Book of Mormon, Doctrine and Covenants, and Pearl of Great Price all acknowledge the existence of Satan. So Latter-day Saints cannot in good faith deny Satan's role in human experience.

But the question is: How can we contend with or withstand Satan? I maintain that we should treat him as though he did not exist or, in other words, ignore him. There is no way that we can build a constructive relationship with him. He is utterly untrustworthy. Jesus said, "Get thee behind me, Satan." I say, "To hell with Satan!" Leave him alone in his own territory.

Nephi, speaking of the Millennium when Christ will reign, tells us how Satan can be bound.

> And because of the righteousness of his [Christ's] people, Satan has no power; wherefore, he cannot be loosed for the space of many years; for he hath no power over the hearts of the people, for they dwell in righteousness. (1 Ne. 22:26)

So we must look elsewhere for the strength and wisdom to eliminate things which diminish our lives.

Another unprofitable way of coping with our weaknesses, I believe, is to deal with the sources of the problems directly. For example, if one is overweight and wishes to reduce, there is little value in thinking about food. Even adopting and adhering to a specific diet seldom suffices. Likewise the alcoholic gains little, if any, strength to overcome his problem by fighting liquor directly, by visualizing a glass of champagne before him. The man who is lustful will not overcome his state of mind or action by contemplating or even fighting in his imagination the attractive forms of women. Or if one loses his/her temper in family relations, it is not enough to combat it with no reinforcement beyond a desire to change. I have read of people addicted to drugs or cigarettes who kept some on themselves to prove their own strength but eventually succumbed to the temptation.

How then do we change our undesirable attitudes, actions, and habits? I learned long ago that all behavior is caused. We do things to gain some satisfaction. To quit one type of behavior, we must find substitutes. For example, people may overeat for lack of fulfillment in other areas of living. If they could achieve in one area of life, athletics or aerobics for instance, their self-control in regard to food would increase. Alcoholics Anonymous has helped many people overcome the drinking problem by sharing fellowship, giving mutual support, and encouraging religious devotion. The Twelve-Step program has been found enormously helpful in other areas of addiction as well.

The ways of helping us overcome our dissatisfactions are varied and multiple, and they differ from person to person. But I am convinced that there is no strength in weakness or in sin. To overcome either, we need to commit ourselves to things that bring us satisfaction and strength.

One of the best ways is to make our Christian faith truly operational. Amulek, in the Book of Mormon, said of Jesus:

> And thus he shall bring salvation to all those who shall believe on his name; this being the intent of this last sacrifice, to bring about the bowels of mercy, which overpowereth justice, and bringeth about means unto men that they may have faith unto repentance. (Alma 34:15)

Faith in Christ and his teachings and service to him and others can give us motivation and strength to rise above weaknesses and sins. A man once confessed a serious sin to me, a sin that weighed him down with great remorse. "How can I be pure of heart again?" he cried. I gave him the privilege of preparing the sacrament at the Lord's table which he carried out faithfully and reverently each Sunday. After a few months he came to me rejoicing and said, "I am a new person. My thoughts are where I want them to be."

Discipleship of Christ, expressed through service to him and others, will give us the desire and strength to change our outlook and our behavior, to cope with aspects of our lives that trouble us. Whatever we put at the center of our lives does *indeed* become our center.

Living Life with Simplicity

We live in a complex, changing society. We are made aware of it daily through the media: television, radio, newspapers, magazines. Numerous organizations—PTAs, churches, private groups and clubs, nonprofit charities, other worthy causes invite affiliation. City dwellers have few chores for their children to do, adding to the difficulties of rearing a family. Also ours has always been a highly mobile society. Moving and adjusting to a new environment is an arduous task which many families experience repeatedly. It is easy to become entangled in things related to moving and to feel as though one's life is out of control, is not one's own.

One key way to cope with complexity is to simplify our interests, commitments, attitudes, obligations, and actions. It is important to make our own choices and not let them be determined by the wishes and requests of others. This calls for reflection and a clarification of our genuine values and interests. In the last analysis it is most important to please ourselves, to keep our own integrity. It is too easy to be concerned about what other people might think of us. To try to please everyone is a sure way to diminish our own sense of self.

Life is difficult and stressful if we feel the necessity of "keeping up with the Joneses." I heard a Relief Society president of modest means tell her husband of the beautifully furnished homes of sisters she had visited during the day. He felt, with or without cause, the burden of providing comparable furnishings for their home. His wife, if envious enough, might have left the home to work merely to provide the "things" she coveted.

Luxurious living is not necessarily good living. A well-to-do couple had their house fixed with every thinkable mechanical and electrical device. They were called out of state for a few years, and their son and his wife moved in. They had nothing but troubles and expenses keeping all the technological gadgets operational.

There is a Chinese saying: "Wealth is an invitation to robbery" and, we might add, to envy. The Chinese also say: "He is rich who has the fewest wants." I like that statement. Contentment removes much pressure and anxiety from living. True, we need some essentials such as food, shelter, utilities, and health care. And human beings enjoy living with beauty. But while they are absolutely essential, they are not the things of ultimate worth.

We need to spend time and means on things that matter most such as the quality of our relationships in the family, in marriage, in religion, in the neighborhood. This takes time and requires reflection and meditation.

We humans are blessed with brains, with minds. We can't understand everything or anything of importance completely, but we need to exercise our minds. One way is to concentrate mainly on a single subject and study it regularly until we feel knowledgeable and at home in that area. My father used to talk about simple living and high thinking. Thinking is within reach of everyone. It costs little and anchors one in life.

A thoughtful wife and excellent housekeeper of my acquaintance said, "Put on the level of routine everything that belongs there." I suppose she meant that we should not spend thought and energy deciding if and when we should do the chores that must be done. We should do the dishes, vacuum the rugs, and wash clothes on schedule with a minimum of strong feeling or exercising of the mind. This applies also to shaving, showering, and getting the garbage out to the street, as well as to our jobs anywhere.

We need to save the heart and mind for creative things, for fine human relationships, for playing or listening to good music, for conversation, for reading, for visiting the sick and afflicted. We need to set aside time for a few very worthwhile things—even for solitude and play—and then follow through. This will give us a sense of control and purpose in living.

Likewise we need to give thought to what movements and organizations we join, to be sure they serve some value to ourselves and/or someone else. We may also wish to become a member of one group that is meaningfully involved in the larger society.

In short, we must decide on a few basic values in life and how and when to cultivate them. Then let these form the framework and focus of our lives. From them we can derive meaning and value. We can keep in control. If we believe in God, we can seek his guidance but let no one else determine the course of our life.

Seeking Improvement, Not Perfection

One evening at the close of a fireside, a young mother came to me and said: "I am supposed to be a perfect wife, a perfect mother, a perfect neighbor, homemaker, and church worker; and I am none of these. What am I to do? I'm frustrated."

I said to her, "Don't try to be perfect in this life. Be a good mother, a cheerful wife, a reasonably good housekeeper, a conscientious church worker." Why should I give her this advice when so much is said in the Mormon church and in the scriptures about being perfect, about perfecting the Saints? I believe in using *perfect* as a verb, seeking to improve our lives and using Jesus as our model. But thinking of perfection as a noun and aspiring to reach a state of perfection in this life is fraught with difficulties. Let me point these out and then suggest a better way to live. I have five reasons why I think it is folly to strive for perfection—a state of being which allows for no growth or further development.

First, we cannot define perfection when referring to the spirit—vs. the letter—of religious living. I ascribe perfection to God and to Christ, but I do not fully understand their moral attributes, their thinking, their aspirations. Isaiah makes this clear, speaking for the Lord:

> For my thoughts are not your thoughts, neither are your ways my ways, saith the Lord.
>
> For as the heavens are higher than the earth, so are my ways higher than your ways, and my thoughts than your thoughts. (Isa. 55:8-9)

A second reason why it is unwise to seek perfection is that we are bound to fail. Being human, we err and sin and fall short of our ideal aspirations. Like babies learning to walk, we invariably stumble and fall.

This leaves us with a sense of guilt, a burden of shame and disappointment. A certain amount of remorse is good for us. It may lead to an admission of wrongdoing and repentance; but too much can enervate and discourage us, as illustrated by the remarks of the young mother at the fireside.

A third and serious reason for not seeking perfection is this: We may think we are succeeding! Nothing is more destructive of virtue than consciousness of our virtue, pride in the quality of our lives. Jesus

> spake this parable unto certain which trusted in themselves that they were righteous, and despised others:
>
> Two men went up into the temple to pray; the one a Pharisee, and the other a publican.
>
> The Pharisee stood and prayed thus with himself, God, I thank thee, that I am not as other men are, extortioners, unjust, adulterers, or even as this publican.

> I fast twice in the week, I give tithes of all that I possess.
>
> And the publican, standing afar off, would not lift up so much as his eyes unto heaven, but smote upon his breast, saying, God be merciful to me a sinner.
>
> I tell you, this man went down to his house justified rather than the other: for everyone that exalteth himself shall be abased; and he that humbleth himself shall be exalted. (Luke 18: 9–14)

Striving for perfection puts us on the horns of a dilemma. If we think we are succeeding, we run the risk of losing humility; if we know we are failing, we become discouraged. There is a better way, as I shall indicate later.

A fourth reason I have against pursuing perfection as a goal is my high regard for that unique and exciting doctrine of the LDS religion—eternal progression. Progression means the act of stepping forward. *Eternal* has two meanings: everlasting and godlike. So we believe that we can learn, create, and enlarge life everlastingly in the footsteps of our Creator. I see no stagnation or dead ends ahead, certainly not in our mortal state, and have every hope that even in a celestial hereafter we can continue to improve.

My final reason for not pursuing perfection as a goal is that it narrows our perspective of life. I once had a fine student, a college freshman, who spent much of his time keeping track of himself. He kept several large notebooks in which he recorded his every thought, feeling, and deed. Quite innocently, he lived a self-centered life. Moreover, self-centered perfectionists make themselves insufferable in the eyes of others.

Jesus said that he who would save his life shall lose it, and he who would lose his life for my sake shall find it. Growth towards the elusive and far distant goal of perfection is a by-product of seeking other goals—of living the Christian virtues of humility, integrity, and love.

In seeking to dissuade people from trying to be perfect here and now, how do we interpret Jesus' statement from the Sermon on the Mount: "Be ye therefore perfect, even as your Father which is in heaven is perfect" (Matt. 5:48)? The footnote of Matthew 5:48 tells us that the word *perfect* is translated from the Greek word that means "complete, finished, fully developed"—not possible while we are still "in transit."

Years ago, a student of mine at the Institute of Religion adjacent to the University of Utah suggested that this verse should be read in context. Jesus had been talking about God's impartial love in the preceding verses and was encouraging his disciples to be more loving. A similar passage in Luke states: "Be ye therefore merciful, as your Father also is merciful" (6:36). The New English Bible translation of Matt. 5:48 reads: "Let there be no limit to your goodness even as the goodness of god knows no bounds." These admonitions are appealing and much more manageable than trying to achieve the impossible goal of perfection in this life.

Even Jesus, to whom we so readily ascribe perfection, did not consider himself perfect, according to the writers of the Gospels:

> And when he [Jesus] was gone forth into the way, there came one running, and kneeled to him, and asked him, Good Master, what shall I do that I may inherit eternal life?
>
> And Jesus said unto him, Why callest thou me good? there is none good but one, that is, God. (Mark 10:17-18)

This view of perfection helps us to focus our attention on the possible instead of expending our energies in frustrating attempts to achieve the impossible. It can help us cope better by harnessing our strengths to deal with the difficulties of life instead of berating ourselves for falling short of perfection.

Adapted from chapter 8 of *I Believe*, Lowell L. Bennion, Salt Lake City: Deseret Book, 1983. Used by permission.

Living Life in Day-Tight Compartments

Many of us try to deal with the whole of life—the past, present, and future—all at once. This can become an overwhelming burden, too much for us to carry. At the same time we regret our past sins and failures, and we fear that our plans and dreams for the future will not materialize. Life is more fulfilling and less stressful if we make peace with the past, daydream less about the future, and enjoy each day as it comes.

One of Shakespeare's most memorable heroines is Lady Macbeth, whose sanity wavers under the weight of the crime she has urged her husband to commit. Seeing her wandering, lost in her own world of madness and obsession, Macbeth demands of the doctor:

> Canst thou not minister to a mind diseased,
> Pluck from the memory a rooted sorrow,
> Raze out the written troubles of the brain
>
> And with some sweet oblivious antidote,
> Cleanse the stuff'd bosom of that perilous stuff
> Which weighs upon the heart? (5.iii.41-46)

What can we do about the burdensome aspects of our past? Is there any way to change or eradicate them? I believe there is. We can reinterpret the past. Though we cannot change a single event or undo what is done, the past as a whole is ever-changing. It is not a fixed thing. Each day we live, we add to it. And, depending on how we live, we enrich or debase our past to some degree.

Elizabeth Barrett Browning wrote:

> Let no man till his death be called unhappy,
> Measure not the work
> Until the day's out and the labour done.

My wife and I lost our first child, a beautiful, happy baby girl. The experience devastated us and burdened our days with grief. But rather than let such a loss claim our emotional energy, we chose to go onward, focused on the future, even though we had little heart for it. In hope and courage, we conceived another child. Eventually, we had four sons and another daughter, all healthy, interesting children. As we experienced joy with our living children, the tragedy of our first loss receded from the foreground of our lives. Against the growing context of our lives, we have been able to remember her with more love than grief and relive the brief joy we knew with her.

Repentance also can change the sins of the past, giving an entirely new meaning to our lives.

> Therefore, O thou son of man, speak unto the house of Israel . . . saying, If our transgressions and our sins be upon us, and we pine away in them, how should we then live?

> Say unto them, as I live, saith the Lord God, I have no pleasure in the death of the wicked; but that the wicked turn from his way and live. . . .
>
> Again, when I say unto the sicked, Thou shalt surely die; if he turn from his sin, and do that which is lawful and right;
>
> If the wicked restore the pledge, give again that he had robbed, walk in the statutes of life, without committing iniquity; he shall surely live, he shall not die.
>
> None of his sins that he hath committed shall be mentioned unto him: he hath done that which is lawful and right; he shall surely live. (Ezek. 33:10-11, 14-16)

I have always been moved by the Savior's three famous parables about God's love and forgiveness: the lost sheep, the lost coin, and the prodigal (lost) son (see Luke 15). The earthly father in the prodigal son parable represents our Heavenly Father. The boy's father watched for his son, ran out to meet him, fell on his neck, kissed him, and rejoiced because he was found. Repentance brings complete forgiveness by Deity and reveals the great love and grace of Christ.

Even when our past has been relatively free of sin and sorrow, there is little point in spending too much time reliving its memory. Sometimes the past seems better than the present because we tend to forget some of its difficulties. This, too, is a dangerous place to dwell, for it saps our courage to face present difficulties and reduces our joy in the present. We are living in the present, and we must make that our focus.

Similarly, it seems unwise to throw our energies into the future and develop strong expectations of what life will be like when we reach some perfect but not yet realized point. If life has taught me anything, it is that our futures are uncertain. Life may bring us great joy or heartbreaking sorrow. Our only access to the future, and the best way to determine in some measure its character, is by what we do today. What does the Savior have to say about worrying about the future? "Take therefore no thought for the morrow: for the morrow shall take thought for the things of itself. Sufficient unto the day is the evil thereof." (Matt. 6:34).

We all have futures, and we should plan for them—for schooling, work, marriage, a family. But after we hope, dream dreams, exercise faith, write down some goals and plan how to reach them, we should then get down to the business of living today, because today is the only fragment of time directly within our control.

If we live well this and each succeeding day, the future will take care of itself. We can learn something daily, offer solace to someone in need, express love to a friend or kin, create something beautiful or worthwhile, listen to uplifting music, or read something thought provoking. Before retiring each evening, we can jot down a few things to do tomorrow to make the day worthwhile, to justify living. Then we can scratch them off as we accomplish them. Or we can keep a journal of the contents of our day.

I have always valued Lehi's advice (given in the present tense) since I first discovered it as a young man: "Men are that they might have joy [here and now]" (2 Ne. 2:25). So are women.

Jesus said likewise: "I am come that they might have life, and that they might have it more abundantly" (John 10:10). Joy and abundant life come from living well in the present, focusing on each day's tasks and each day's satisfactions. Living largely in day-tight compartments can be more rewarding than being preoccupied with the past and/or future.

SECTION FOUR

Matters of the Mind and Spirit

Accepting Yourself as Unique

When I was a young lad growing up in Salt Lake City, I had a friend whose parents came from Germany and who therefore had a German name. One day he said to me, "If my name were Cannon or Ashton"—two respected pioneer names in our neighborhood—"I could be somebody." As it turned out, this German family, whose name was Buehner, made an outstanding name for itself in the Church and the community. They developed a highly respected cement contracting firm. They became bishops and teachers in the Church. The oldest son served as a member of the Presiding Bishopric.

Every human being is conscious of self. There is no escape from this awareness except through severe mental illness. One of the three or four most basic human psychological needs is to feel worthwhile, to enjoy self-esteem. How do we gain this feeling?

One way is to take pride in our uniqueness. Every person is original in some way. An interesting and distinctive trait often becomes difficult and uncomfortable for many people. I recall a five-year-old neighbor struggling to straighten out his red curl—

the envy of every mother in the neighborhood—who wondered over and over again, "Why can't my hair be *straight* like Ben's and Josh's and Travis's?"

Take pride in being yourself. Envy no one; copy no one. Rejoice in your original looks, talents, feelings, and thoughts. Cherish and enhance what you are. That same neighbor is now eighteen and glories in those red curls—and so do his numerous girlfriends!

Don't be afraid to be yourself. Listen to others, read widely, and heed counsel; but do your own thinking, draw your own conclusions, speak your own words, determine your own actions. Yes, in the process you will reveal your ignorance and make mistakes, but you will also grow, learn, and increase in integrity and self-worth. Accept full responsibility for what you feel, think, and do.

I was amazed to hear a fifty-year-old man blame his bad temper on his father, who had been dead for many years. There may have been a point when this man was, as a child, so thoroughly under his father's influence that he could not imagine any other way to meet frustrations than with an explosion of bad temper. But there comes a time when it is useless to blame parents or anyone else for weaknesses or mistakes. Even though we are shaped markedly by our genes and environment, in ways we can't readily measure, it seems folly to excuse our behavior by blaming it on others. To blame is to be stuck, to have a "victim" mentality where there is no moving on or growing.

We were born to function, to be productive, to be creative. We will not feel fulfilled unless we express ourselves in meaningful ways. We don't have to be a Beethoven, Shakespeare, or Michelangelo, nor even a Maurice Abravanel, a Wallace Stegner, or a Georgia O'Keefe. We need to just be ourselves; express our own feelings, imagination, and thoughts; and learn to use our hands. Anyone with the courage to do this can become a creator. I am certainly no Shakespeare, but I think I have had as much satisfaction in shaping my ideas into prose as he did in creating his immortal poetry.

All of us have the power to forge creative relationships. All we need is sincerity and interest in the welfare of others. People need assurance of our respect and acceptance, our interest in what they are doing, and our awareness of their worth as individuals. A teacher has many opportunities to create such relationships with students. Every member of a family has the same potential power. And no one can have too many friends.

Guard against self-pity. Most of us are either too short or too tall, too thin or too fat, too old or too arthritic, bald or prematurely gray, or rather homely by Hollywood standards. We should make a clear distinction between what we can change and what we cannot change. Then we must accept what cannot be changed, either finding value in it or ignoring it. I started to go bald in my twenties and have been completely bald since my early thirties. I waste no time pitying myself, poring over ads for hair replacement, or weighing the merits of toupees. I think of my high and noble brow and of forebears whom I admire who were also bald. I find my head easy to wash and dry. Since women seldom go bald,

I accept my baldness as a witness of my masculinity.

Advantages can be found in most unhappy situations. Financial loss can help us re-evaluate our sense of values. Illness can enhance appreciation for health. Losing an election can free a person to devote more time to family and/or private interests.

When I attended the University of Utah, I used to bet someone a malted milk that Colorado would beat Utah in a football game. I wanted Utah to win; and if they did, I gladly treated my friend. If they lost, I enjoyed my malted milk. I won either way.

We can choose to maximize our uniqueness, avoid self-pity, and take advantage of any negative situation. We need not be defeated twice—once by a given circumstance and then by our attitude toward it. Coping with the world is much easier if we don't have to battle ourselves, too.

Cultivating the Mind

Latter-day Saints often cite Joseph Smith's declaration that "the glory of God is intelligence," but I wonder how often we say to ourselves, "My glory also lies in my intelligence"? What would life be like without the mind? We would be robbed not only of the ability to think, of memory, of ideas, of imagination, but also of many other great experiences which depend on the mind. We could be neither moral nor spiritual without our mental faculties. And what would art and nature mean without the mind? Even the richest aspects of social life—friendship, marriage and family, fraternity, democracy—depend on the ability to share thoughts.

The process of thinking is worthwhile in itself, satisfying our intellectual hunger. Children often display an insatiable curiosity, firing questions without interruption. From birth to death intellectual activity can enhance living in vital ways.

Life, of course, involves more than the mind. We are also creatures of feeling which runs deep in human nature. It seems to be the source of most of our motivation and satisfaction. However, this aspect of life needs the direction and control which the intellect can lend it. Without rich feeling, life becomes cold and joyless; conversely, without thought, feeling may run amuck and defeat itself.

The older we become the more we recognize that our happiness and security lie not so much in the material and physical worlds as they do in the mental and spiritual. Memory grows, and we gain more ideas to relate to one another. Compared to the body, the mind seems indefatigable. It can support us through the infirmities of aging with wisdom and humor. We know men and women in their eighties whose physical output has reached an all-time low, but whose mental life remains rich and rewarding. Only through the mind can we transcend some of the limitations imposed upon us by the body.

INFORMING THE MIND

The mind is like a manufacturing plant. Unless raw material feeds it, nothing of value comes out. That mind functions best which is well fed, other things being equal. Ideas, words, perceptions, and experience are the raw stuff essential to fruitful thinking.

Recent trends in education have emphasized expression, encouraging students to talk freely about every subject under the sun. Expression alone does not cultivate the mind and may even exhaust it. We must also acquire information and ideas—something to talk about—before discussion can develop mental ability and power.

Many of us have a mania to become well read, so we can quote the names of books and authors in conversation. Sometimes the desire to say "I have read this" is stronger than the desire to say "I have learned this." Rather than bluff our way, we should admit freely what we know or do not know, ever learning—

even after graduation, marriage, and retirement. As Confucius warned, "Love of knowing, without the love of learning, leads to dissipation of the mind."

Being well informed has become increasingly difficult in an age exploding with information. Moreover, modern life easily distracts us from study. We are too busily engaged in being entertained or gaining material things to spend much time seeking knowledge. Stadiums, theaters, and highways are full of people day after day while libraries remain half empty, even though smaller in size and fewer in number. As a book publisher once observed,

> These instruments of modern communication [radio and television] are actually more instruments of impact. They require more a passive participation—often none whatsoever. They represent the easier way. They are a substitute—for the lazy mind. There is no time for reflection. One cannot stop to think. One cannot re-read and ponder a paragraph. One grows to take it as it comes. In large part it is a split-second entertainment, addressed primarily to the trigger-happy mind. (*Saturday Review of Literature*, August 18, 1951, inside front cover)

ON BEING WELL READ

It is wise to expose ourselves to many interests and read in several fields. Sometime senior students in engineering, law, or medicine wake up to the realization that they have been moving in a deep and narrow rut. They sense the need for exposure to literature, music, or perhaps international affairs.

Everyone would do well to read in a few areas besides those required by his or her vocation.

While being well rounded has many satisfactions, it remains desirable to become well grounded in one particular field. By becoming both versatile and accomplished—a "Jack" of several trades and a master of one—life becomes more adventurous and secure. A person well trained in one area usually becomes a better student in other areas simply by virtue of having learned how to study and think.

That ability should enhance reading and appreciation of the classics of literature, whether ancient or contemporary. For beauty of expression, richness of human interest, and profitable moral instruction, the Bible is the greatest book we know. Mormon scriptures also contain many passages of literary quality and even more of religious and moral worth. But Latter-day Saints ought to devote at least as much reading time to the classics of other religions and cultures as they do to their own.

CULTIVATING THE IMAGINATION

Imagination is the power of the mind to take single images and put them together into an image that has never existed before. Thus, the imagination forever enriches life with new combinations of ideas, images, and feelings. No real creation can occur in the sciences or the humanities without imagination.

Imagination even plays a role in a prophet's life, leading him to ask questions of God born of a burning desire to know. It helps him to walk by faith. The revelation God gives him is not the working of his own mind, but his imagination prepares him to seek and receive truth from a higher power.

One must understand, of course, the role of imagination in life. It does not substitute for knowledge or truth. It has little to do with idle daydreaming. It is simply a quality of the mind that motivates us to find truth. What we find and live by must always be checked by the usual means of verifying the value of things.

Each of us should let our fancy soar. An eager and active mind becomes pregnant with new insights and hypotheses in any field that attracts its attention. Of such stuff are poets, philosophers, artists, and children made. The imagination can be quickened by listening to youngsters, observing nature and people, and by appreciating and participating in the arts.

The mind resembles a muscle in that its real power comes from regular use. To read and meditate privately is essential but not enough. We should become eagerly engaged in discussions with friends and teachers through the medium of ideas. Taking full advantage of opportunities to speak and write about our ideas will help us cultivate the mind.

In any group or in any speech given or lesson prepared, often the most relished gift is that of a new idea. It can enliven a discussion and expand our lives like little else. A new idea is like sun after rain, something to make all else grow.

Adapted from Lowell L Bennion's "Goals for Living" manual, 1952, Chapter IX.

Enjoying the Arts

Art, like religion, is universal in human experience. In almost any culture one could name, people have danced, drawn pictures, told stories, sung songs, woven baskets, or otherwise expressed themselves artistically. Something so ubiquitous arouses our curiosity. What is art, and why do humans show such great interest in it? What values can its cultivation bring to our lives? Why should we try to improve our ability to appreciate and create one or more of the arts—architecture, dancing, literature, music, painting, sculpture, theater?

Let us confess at the outset that in discussing art and aesthetic experience we are treading on professional ground. I cannot claim any real artistic aptitude, and my limited level of appreciation I owe largely to the influence of my wife and study group friends. Even among professionals we find divergent opinions about basic artistic principles. Since the arts rest more on feeling than thought, they do not lend themselves to description as readily as things we can measure. Our purpose here is simply to suggest, in simple terms, a few important notions about the nature of the arts.

As a human creation, a work of art is presented to the eye or ear through the medium of some semi-permanent material such as paper, pigment, stone, or wood. Its concrete form distinguishes art clearly from other objects. Its creation and contemplation bring to both the artist and the appreciator what is called "aesthetic feeling."

Any work of art consists of two elements:

(1) stimuli absorbed by artists from their environs;

(2) their reworking of these impressions through their minds and feelings.

A particular product bears the distinctive stamp of the artist. A certain quality pervades the entire work no matter how varied or detailed its parts. This unity reflects the character and genius of its creator.

A landscape painting, for instance, is inspired by what the artist sees in nature. He or she, however, recreates the vista. Some elements are added to it, others left out—resulting in a simplified but more unified scene. The size of the canvas and frame set the painting off from the rest of nature. The piece of art takes on a more permanent quality compared to the changing natural scene. Art thus acquires some advantages over nature as an object for human contemplation and enjoyment. In its more concrete and lasting form, we can return to it again and again. Artists see, hear, and feel things that we who are less sensitive fail to perceive. They thereby articulate important aspects of life for the rest of us.

AESTHETIC EXPERIENCE

Aesthetic means the opposite of *an*aesthetic. Anyone undergoing surgery appreciates an anaesthetic which brings loss of sensation and feeling.

Aesthetic experience involves just the opposite—emotions or moods that enable us to apply our senses. As feelings, aesthetics differ in significant ways from such emotional experiences of life as fear, jealousy, or romantic love. Let us consider some of these differences.

In aesthetic experience, we identify ourselves with the art object. We can listen to a symphony and lose ourselves, forgetting all about associates, responsibilities, perhaps even the hardness of the bench on which we are sitting. Many emotional experiences become centered in us, but the arts can leave us quite unaware of our own emotions, drawing our interest away from ourselves. Afterwards, when once again aware of ourselves, we feel wonderfully refreshed.

Aesthetic experience is purely contemplative, leading to no immediate action. Just to listen or look is wholly satisfying, as in true worship. We also entertain a make-believe attitude. Realizing that a tragedy on stage is only a make-believe re-creation of a real-life situation, we do not scream when Othello stabs Desdemona. Tragedy in life enervates or tears us apart, but experiencing it on stage leaves us reflective.

In aesthetic creation and appreciation, we endow objects with human values. We speak of pictures or sculptures as graceful, warm, or harmonious. Art objects arouse the qualities of our nature, and we, in turn, identify them with what we see or hear.

CONTRIBUTIONS OF ARTS TO LIFE

The arts cultivate the "feeling" aspect of life. We may want to apologize for feelings associated with such vices as anger, envy, and vanity. But feelings also provide us with deep-seated satisfactions and motivate us to act in positive ways. Even the joy of intellectual achievement is *felt*.

Aesthetic experience is particularly valuable as a unifying process. Our minds are usually in a state of flux. Contemplating or creating art enables us to forget the things that we normally fret about and become more at one with ourselves. Art can relieve us of our burdens by getting them out into the open and by enabling us to view them from a more objective perspective. Reading the Book of Job, for example, has brought consolation to countless people. Job's experience makes suffering seem bearable, even beautiful.

The arts provide us with a marvelous channel of self-expression. Feelings need expression of a kind that will neither injure nor destroy us. Self-expression becomes as vital to mental and emotional health as self-control. The arts offer us a safety-valve, a means of releasing the tensions of life. A blind John Milton expressed himself more powerfully in *Paradise Lost* than he could have done in real life. And think of Beethoven, stone-deaf, producing his last symphonies. All of us have more to give the world than we might imagine, since the arts impose few, if any, restrictions on our efforts to voice our joys and sorrows.

Cultivating the arts can help us in other walks of life. A Sunday School teacher had tried for days to organize a lesson that would appeal to her class. She was confident that her plan was sound, but it remained vague. On Friday night she went to a piano concert which moved her so deeply that she forgot all about her class. Afterwards her vision cleared and a strategy for presenting the lesson took shape. It seemed as if her mind worked better after being relaxed by the strains of Chopin and Debussy.

The cultivation of anything good should have an uplifting influence on life as a whole. A cultivated mind, as we have seen, can enrich the moral and spiritual life of everyone. Feeling cultivated through the arts can make us more sensitive in human relations and also prepare us to worship God. Much of the world's greatest art has been inspired of religion and has, in turn, greatly enriched religious feeling and living.

Thus far we have discussed the arts and our relationship to them in a rather abstract way to provide perspective. But the best way to enjoy the arts is by immediate experience with them. Given the highly subjective nature of aesthetic expression, our capacities to cultivate it will vary greatly, but a few suggestions may increase our involvement in the arts no matter what our particular interest.

First of all, don't expect to enjoy all arts or all expressions of the same art. We simply are not versatile or trained enough to respond to the manifold creations of all cultures and ages. Be encouraged and satisfied if you delight in one part of any art.

Be sincere enough to admit to yourself, if not to others, that you've had no aesthetic reaction to some artistic activity. Don't wait to read a critic's assessment of a book, concert, or play before expressing your own opinion.

Expose yourself with patience and without prejudice to the arts. As a new missionary I was taken to hear Wagner's *Lohengrin* one night in Cologne, Germany. The opera lasted three and one-half hours. Apart from the "Overture" and the "Wedding March," I appreciated little of the long performance. But I kept attending an opera once or twice a month even though I had no time for any formal study of music.

Toward the end my mission, I invited another young missionary to hear the same *Lohengrin* with me, produced this time in Zurich, Switzerland. The new elder, who liked to sing and sang well, walked away so bored that he vowed never to go to another opera. I may have grinned a bit with sympathy, recalling my own similar response two years earlier. But I marveled at how much watching thirty or forty operas had enhanced my own appreciation of that art form. For two or three days after the performance I could still feel Wagner's music welling up within me.

Finally, let me urge you to become a participant! One of my four sons, when he was about ten years old and glued to radio serials for home entertainment, became much annoyed when his parents insisted on listening to one or two symphonic programs during the week. On Saturdays, when he wanted to hear a football game, his mother tried with little success to talk him into listening to live Metropolitan Opera broadcasts. He complained quite a bit about these intrusions of dull "classical stuff" on his exciting programs.

And then something strange happened. He began playing the tuba. In junior high school his band teacher (Ormand Weight) had him playing simplified excerpts from sundry symphonies. Our son became even more enamored of classical music when he began taking piano lessons. When he tired of practicing he listened to records on the phonograph.

When he attended college he subscribed to Utah Symphony concerts, outstripping his parents in their devotion to music and chiding his younger brothers for their lack of appreciation. In his case, participation clearly, if gradually, made a big difference in his feelings about music as an art. Joy and aesthetic satisfaction are waiting expectantly for each of us—a gift to all those who give any art ample time and energy.

A ten-year-old once wrote a poem about writing a poem. She said in the style of a child,

> . . . In many of my poems I talk about a heartbeat.
> Weather it be of a baby, a fire, a bird, an aspin, or a stream,
> A heartbeat reprecents life,
> And life are what my poems are all about.
> After you've written a poem,
> The walls are alive, the rug's a live, the whole room's alive,
> And sentences start popping into your head . . .
>
> Meagan T. Heath

Enjoying any of the arts can bring that same aliveness into *your* life. To miss such feasting would be like denying food to a hungry child. It can be the heartbeat that signals well-being in mind, body, and spirit.

Adapted from Lowell L. Bennion's "Goals for Living," manual, Chap. XIX, 1952.

Being Creative in Life

A father plowed, harrowed and leveled an acre of land for a pasture. One day, while he was away, his young son and his friends played war in the middle of the fields, building tunnels, an observation tower, and trenches. The father, a bit perturbed, but sympathetic with a boy's need for activity, asked his son to dig near the house and not in a field ready to be planted. There was plenty of uncultivated land about the house.

A night or two later the father led a friend across the front lawn in the dark and they both fell into a pit. The boy and his pals had taken him at his word and had dug near the house.

The father concluded that human nature was like water—it must run in one direction or another. If dammed off in one place, it will break out in another. The father determined to help his boy dig foundations instead of leaving him to dig pits.

We are all like that boy. We, too, were born to dig. A baby must function. One of our very few innate fears is that of being restricted in movement. Every human being desires to function, to have expression. We have drives, imagination, curiosity, and aspirations which compel us to act to satisfy our nature. In our beginnings, our very nature forbids us to be indifferent and passive. We must dig all the time, even in sleep when the subconscious is active. Even shy people, who seek the shadow, are busily engaged in introspection. Passivity, if developed, comes through passive experience, like sitting for hours before a television screen and being acted upon rather than being active.

The question is not *whether* we shall function, but only *how* shall we function? How shall we give vent to this tremendous urge to live? Shall we fill our days with trivialities, routine, daydreaming? Or can we learn to express our natures more significantly by engaging more often in creative living?

Each of us has a great need to be creative. Creativeness satisfies our hunger and thirst for meaning. It brings joy. It is a quality that can enter into and enhance anything we do with our hands, hearts, and minds. It is a worthwhile goal to consider and to pursue.

TO BE CREATIVE ONE MUST EXPERIENCE SOMETHING NEW

We need the feeling of discovery, of invention, of originality. A new idea, new sensations, animated feelings emerge in our consciousness. Habit, routine, copying, and imitation contain a minimum of creative experience because one feels nothing novel.

In contrast to being creative, addiction to television can deprive people of real-life experience. Too much television watching weakens identity and true self-esteem. It can condition watchers to unreality as it habituates them to a desire for repetitive over-stimulation. Adults as well as children can become accustomed to immediate gratification without significant personal effort and interaction with others. Too much television can take the life and vitality out of people and their communities. What could be more dead-end than the passivity of soulless, heartless, and even mindless watchers of whatever is fed them from the selection of strangers?

On the other hand, the process, the activity involved in the vital creative experience, is not a dead-end product. Creativeness lies within the creator, not in the creation, which is only the witness and memory of creativeness. The young woman or man who arrives, independently, at an ingenious color scheme for a college apartment feels wonderfully creative and is so, even though that student may find afterwards that a similar design appeared two years ago in a magazine. The same creative feeling could hold true for an author writing a book or an attorney constructing ways to serve a client, a teacher presenting exciting projects to a class, a builder with a new design for a fireplace, or a quilter with a new idea for a pattern.

To get a new idea, to see ideas in new relationships, to build something original on paper or with one's hands, to discover or produce something new through one's own thinking—to thus use the imagination or intuition is to be creative.

ALL CREATION REFLECTS THE CHARACTER OF ITS CREATOR

The universe, in all of its beauty, vastness, orderliness, and awesomeness, is a reflection of the mind and will of God, as witnessed in the scriptures frequently. For example:

> The earth rolls upon her winds, and the sun giveth his light by day, and the moon giveth her light by night, and the stars also give their light, as they roll upon their winds in their glory, in the midst of the power of God.
>
> Unto what shall I liken these kingdoms, that ye may understand?
>
> Behold, all these are kingdoms, and any man who hath seen any or the least of these hath seen God moving in his majesty and power. (D&C 88:45-47)

When we live creatively our creations also reflect our own feelings, values, ideas, hopes, and hands. The Egyptians of old reflected their static, eternal view of things in their pyramids and sphinxes; the Greeks revealed their mobility of mind, their sense of balance and proportion, their love of life in their architecture and sculpture. In our own creative moments we, too, express our individuality. We feel the power of our minds. We delight in the range of our imagination, in the depth of feeling, in the variety or intensity of sensory perception. Creativity means participation—eager, active, often exultant participation in life.

IN CREATION WE FEEL UNIFIED

We become aware of ourselves. Feeling and thought work harmoniously together. Every avenue of life seems all at once to lead somewhere, to fit into a meaningful whole. Creation is a qualitative experience of the highest order, bringing into activity the whole person. In contrast, copying, repeating, reiterating, living by the input of others, though at times necessary and useful, are usually undertaken quantitatively and rather mechanically.

Becoming a mother or father, particularly with a purposeful and positive attitude toward the process, embodies all the qualities of creativeness. Both parents have produced something new and wholly original. There have been billions of babies born, but none like this one. Especially for the mother, but also true for an expectant father, this is an entirely unique venture. Their thoughts, feelings, and sensations are so personal they cannot be communicated adequately to anyone else. The child bears the stamp of both parents. Their very life force has entered into its being. For the mother, it has issued from her body as well as from her mind and heart. Having the wanted baby, even when difficult, she has felt wonderfully whole in this creation of a child. Her physical, mental, moral, and spiritual life have all come into play together. Childbirth has required faith, hope, courage, and love as well as struggle, pain, suffering, and effort from her and in many ways from her husband—all of these things and more in a single experience.

While acquiring a new baby for a man cannot be the same, his sense of creativity can be quickened as in no other experience. Today a father is invited, in fact urged, to participate in the process. Not only in conception does he pass himself on in his genes, but in the pregnancy he is offered qualified instruction on how the growing proceeds and how to understand what is happening for his wife. He can attend classes to help her in labor, to attend the birth of his child as more than someone waiting outside. The birth itself can be as thrilling for him as it is for her. Then, attending to the baby can be his opportunity for seeing the miracle of growth. No longer does fathering exclude either parent from accepting creative responsibility for, caring for, teaching, and showing love for the child. In life there can be no greater opportunity for creativeness than in parenting.

Any creativity draws on our uniqueness. No two people have the same inborn inclinations or the training inherent in growing up in a given family, place, historical setting, geographical environment, cultural or religious circumstances. But we all are human and interrelated. Our power to think and feel and do can be encouraged within ourselves as well as by outside forces.

MANY THINGS CAN DESTROY CREATIVENESS

Our grandfathers raced their own horses or rode in the rodeo on the 4th of July. Today we go to the fair and pay to see professionals ride other people's horses. Or, even more sedentary, we watch on television as sports have become highly commercialized—football, baseball, tennis, and basketball, for instance. Even though women now can compete in team sports in high schools and universities, most students do not engage actively in sports but pay to watch one to five percent of their classmates play for the glory of their alma mater. A century ago people in many parts of the world—and those in the LDS church in particular—entertained themselves and one another, or went without entertainment. Today children huddle before the TV or wear headphones, listen to CDs, or fix their eyes on a computer screen and play video games, or they go to a movie or a sports event. What time is alloted or need felt to participate creatively in drama, music, or play? How much more interest and self-control are needed to forsake these modern attractions for piano practice or creative study than formerly?

In the '60s an astute European visited America for a year. He liked Americans and their amazing country. After visiting a number of movies and observing people's reactions, however, he concluded that they went there so often and in such large numbers to win by reflection and vicariously the affection, adventure, and genuine achievement that were so lacking in their own lives.

WE LIVE IN AN AGE OF GADGETS

Science has enabled us to produce countless gadgets and technological servants. Ingenious manufacturers, advertisers, and salespeople have combined forces to make us feel uncomfortable if we don't own and display our share. Many are useful. For most of them we are thankful, but they do stand in the way of the average person's creativity. Why make anything that can be purchased so easily ready-made?

Years ago, on a ranch isolated by bad roads and 100 miles of desert, when a wagon tongue broke, it was replaced by one hewn for the occasion out of the limb of a tree, by a sixteen-year-old boy with an ax, hatchet, and knife. He faced a problem and resolved it with his own ingenuity and hands. He felt vital to the operation of the ranch, anything but expendable, as many of our teenagers feel today.

There is another side to this story. Our mechanical age has freed us from much drudgery—has put power and the possibility of leisure time into our hands. The question is: Do we use this added leisure in creative activity or do we work all the harder in order to buy cars and power lawn mowers which will save us time? A friend put it this way: "We keep working as hard as we can to buy more and more things so we won't have to work as hard."

Mark Twain said: "Civilization is a limitless multiplication of unnecessary necessities." (*Reader's Digest*, November 1951, p. 106)

WE LIVE IN AN AGE OF SPECIALIZATION—OF DIVISION OF LABOR.

This has greatly increased production and raised the standard of living immensely. Through it, however, many people spend their working days in uncreative tasks. We met a man in Vienna who, before World War I, had made shoes and boots for princes and peasants. Each pair was a work of art—the fruit of his ideas, his planning, his hands. His mind, heart, and physical energy went into the shoe and with the shoe. His work occupied the entire man. When we knew him he worked in a shoe factory where he performed one minor operation on hundreds of shoes each day. Those shoes belonged to no one. His contribution was anonymous. He was brokenhearted to be thus reduced to uncreative anonymity. Something wonderful had gone out of his life.

What can be done about it? Can we roll time

back or stand in the way of the economic reality that mass production is more efficient? Can we stifle the onrushing use of computers to sit in front of to solve our problems and divide us into those who know how to use them and those who don't? No. Either we must choose vocations which are creative or find creative outlets for life in extra work activities made possible by our technological age.

WE LIVE IN AN AGE OF EXPERTS

We each have our own field of knowledge and skill. There was a day when an educated person knew almost everything that was known. Later there was a time when a physician knew all the medicine that was known. Then came the eye, ear, nose, and throat specialist. Now we have those who specialize just in the eye or even in the diseases of the eye or eye surgery, or a doctor who tends only to dizziness caused by inner ear problems. Who dares to do one's own thinking in this highly complex age of experts and specialists? It was a rare and refreshing experience to meet an uneducated farmer the other day who said, with more confidence than an expert, "I knows what I know and I knows what I don't know." I am not decrying experts. We need them, but they often frighten the average person out of courage to do some creative thinking, too.

WE LIVE IN A MASS AGE

In many places in our time the individual feels that it's possible to count for little. Armies fight battles in mass movements or from a foreign sky. An individual feels ineffectual in political life as one voter in thousands or millions where the only influential campaign donations are made by wealthy groups with common expectations of repayment in favors by elected officials. We drive the same kind of car as two million others, many of them made in faraway countries.

We live in a great day, but in a day when we are perhaps more hindered than encouraged to be creative. Let us therefore look at the other side of the ledger.

OPPORTUNITIES TO DEVELOP CREATIVENESS

Creativeness is a matter of attitude more than circumstance. To illustrate this point, let us relate two recent conversations about school teaching. One revealed uncreative, the other creative teaching. A friend told us that his five-year-old son came home and said he couldn't stand his teacher because she shouted at him all day. The father visited the class and agreed with his son. The teacher gained the "attention" of the children by out-shouting them.

We rode home with another teacher who revealed her creativeness as she said, "When I have a rowdy child in class, I figure it's my responsibility to engage him or her in something too interesting to resist. If I can get that one child to pay attention, I don't have to worry nearly so much about interesting the rest. They just come along." This thoughtful, creative teacher knew that what matters in a classroom is not what is being taught, but what is being learned.

REJOICE IN YOUR INDIVIDUALITY AND MAKE THE MOST OF IT

God made everything in nature, including each one of us, unique. If we are but sincere in our thinking and behavior, we will think and act as no one else can. We will sense our own originality and find interest and satisfaction in it.

In each of us are talents, abilities, characteristics, and qualities which make us creative if we will have faith sufficient to develop and use them constructively.

We had occasion to call on an English lady the other morning. She had lived in Utah only a few months. She had a husband and five children. They were renting a modest, old home. As we approached the door we heard her singing and conversing with two tiny children while she was doing a large washing. She came to the door, heard something fall in the living room, went to see what had happened, and returned to say: "My little girl just spilled a whole bottle of milk on the living room rug. Excuse me please while I wipe it up. By now, I have a system—just blot and wring—not necks," she laughed. Such a job would have to be enormously frustrating, but she seemed able to move beyond the frustration with equanimity born of a basic love of her children and acceptance of the need for her creative approach ninety per cent of the time in raising children.

LEARN TO BE CREATIVE IN EVERYDAY LIFE

Sometimes we begin to think that all knowledge and wisdom are in schools and libraries or in computers. We cease to be alert and creative in our relationship with people and with nature. One day I was visiting a student who was home on vacation from an Eastern medical school where he was one of the top in his class. While we were talking, his father, who raised chickens, came up the walk with a basket full of eggs. I asked, "May I buy three or four dozen?"

"Surely, I'll get them ready," the father answered.

When it came time to pay him, I found that he was charging me only the wholesale price for large eggs, but had picked out and given me super-colossal eggs. He refused to take more money. When he left us, I said to his son, who had studied religion in my classes, "How does your father get that way?" (The father had had no college education and had spent most of his life as a foreman in coal mines.)

The medic replied quickly and good-humoredly, "Religion comes naturally to my father. He doesn't have to take classes from you to learn it."

I liked that. As I have become better acquainted with the father, I have found a lot of things coming naturally to him. He uses his head. He can repair everything in the house or on his chicken farm. In his relations with people—neighbors, customers, his own large family—he is utterly sincere, simple, direct. He creates new methods in his work and good feeling among those he associates with. His whole relationship to life illustrates how we can be creative in the common experiences of living.

After all, books, works of art, the scriptures, homes and gardens are only the fruit of creativity. Their quality lies in the thinking, feeling, and aspiration of all of us and sometimes, too, in the love and creativity of the great Creator himself.

Nature, the arts, and hobbies are wonderful channels for creative activity We can be whole in nature. Nature can be comfort as well as responsive to our mind and hand. Our relationship to the arts can be richly creative whether in appreciation or creation. They are of such a nature that we can periodically identify our whole feeling with them and come out renewed and whole. Hobbies can be creative because our relationship to them is actuated by simple, sincere motives. We wish merely to enjoy them; hence, there is no inhibition. We give ourselves freely and completely to the garden, to painting, to music, writing, or playing sports.

MASTER THE MEDIA

If we gain more knowledge and skill in any field and more rich experience in life, we have more to draw upon in creative activity. One cannot be very creative at the piano before the third lesson. Considerable mechanics acquired through almost monotonous repetition is a prerequisite to creative piano playing. One cannot build a house as a creative experience unless some considerable knowledge and skill are in one's background.

Anything more mature than the creativeness of a child demands acquisition of skills and knowledge and patient building. Fortunately, this building process can be creative in spirit from the outset. Practicing the piano need not be drudgery and the student who uses imagination just to play scales or to memorize times tables will learn much faster and have a more satisfying experience. Creativeness has one basis, then, in education and hard work. The rest of it is perhaps a matter of faith, attitude, and imagination. Even these, however, can be cultivated. The imagination can be quickened by reflection, observation, reading, and conversation.

If we would preserve our individuality and cherish the feeling of living a meaningful life, we could do no better than to have faith in and cultivate our own creative nature.

It is important to remember that we are an eternal self and will always live with that self. Also, each of us is a child of God and has partaken of God's creative nature.

Only when we are creative can we in some way come to know and rejoice in our own souls.

EPILOGUE

Why I Am a Believer: Wellsprings of My Faith

In this concluding essay I shall declare my relationship to religion, which for me is the gospel of Jesus Christ. Some of it, I am confident, rests on knowledge, but much of it, I acknowledge, depends upon faith. There are different ways of knowing: by reasoning, through one's own and others' experience, by intuition, and by the Holy Ghost. Faith also has multiple sources, much the same as knowledge, but they are more difficult to verify.

THREE PRIMARY PRINCIPLES

There are principles of religion which we can know through observation and experience, both by their presence and the consequences of their absence. We can know they are good and life-fulfilling for the individual and society. There are three such ethical-religious principles which embrace many lesser ones. I don't have to exercise faith in them except to motivate myself to practice them. I refer to humility, integrity, and love.

A humble person recognizes his or her limited knowledge and dependence on God and fellow human beings and hungers for knowledge, understanding, and wisdom. Such a person will follow Jesus' admonition and promise:

> Ask, and it shall be given you; seek, and ye shall find; knock, and it shall be opened unto you:
>
> For every one that asketh receiveth; and he that seeketh findeth; and to him that knocketh it shall be opened. (Matt. 7:7–8)

A humble person also recognizes his or her errors and sins and seeks to correct them. Humility does not mean self-deprecation, but the desire to repent of wrongdoing. Self-acceptance, made possible in part by repentance, is a prerequisite of integrity and love.

Jesus made humility the first of his eight Beatitudes. "Blessed are the poor in spirit . . . " All of the others presuppose a humble spirit and attitude.

Jesus exemplified humility in his own life. When a man came to him and called him "Good Master," Jesus replied, "Why callest thou me good? there is none good but one, that is, God" (Matt. 19:17). A humble person does not seek the honors of men but strives to serve others. One of the Savior's last acts was to wash the feet of his disciples to teach them that they were to minister and not be ministered to.

A second fundamental virtue taught by Jesus was integrity. As the word implies, integrity gives one a sense of wholeness and unity, providing identity and security in a great variety of circumstances. Integrity is the glue that holds the spiritual life together. It is the fruit of sincerity, honesty, and moral courage. It knows no pretense, guile, or deception. It presupposes that a person has principles, values, and goals and lives by them. The first four and the sixth Beatitudes are expressions of integrity: humility, repentance, meekness, hungering and thirsting after righteousness, and purity of heart. "Blessed are the poor in spirit . . . they that mourn . . . the meek . . . they which do hunger and thirst after righteousness . . . the pure in heart" (Matt 5:3-6, 8).

Love is the great, all-encompassing social virtue which embraces kindness, patience, tolerance, mercy, forgiveness, forbearance, long-suffering, sacrifice, promoting peace and goodwill. Love is alter-ego centered, seeking the well-being of others, treating people as ends in themselves rather than as means for gratifying one's own needs.

Love is a verb as well as a noun. It becomes most valuable when it tries to meet the needs of others—both material and spiritual. It becomes real when it feeds the hungry, clothes the naked, shelters the homeless, comforts the afflicted, provides warm acceptance, and helps others to find their own worth.

I know that humility, integrity, and love are sound principles of individual and social life. I don't need to exercise faith in them anymore. I need only to practice them and to persuade others, if possible, to live by them. The Apostle Paul said, "If in this life only we have hope in Christ, we are of all men most miserable" (1 Cor. 15:19). The principles Jesus taught are as meaningful for this life as they are for eternal life. If there were no God in heaven and no immortality for human life, humility, integrity, and love would still be principles to live by here and now to find fulfillment.

MY FAITH IN GOD

There are other aspects of religion—very basic ones—in which I have to exercise faith. I refer to such beliefs as the existence of a personal God, the atonement of Jesus Christ, and the immortality of the soul. For these beliefs we have the witness of the Holy Ghost, the light of Christ, and the Spirit of God, the Father, but we have to exercise faith in the reality of these influences. We don't know the reality of these things in the same way we know the meaning and value of the principles we have discussed in the first part of this essay. I gladly walk by faith in God, Christ, and personal immortality and freely admit that I do.

I have faith in the existence of a personal supreme being in the universe. I have neither seen him nor heard his voice. My faith is based on several things: I have a high regard for those prophets who bear witness of him, for Moses, Amos, Hosea, Micah, Isaiah, Jeremiah, Jesus, Paul, and Joseph Smith, among others. I find their descriptions of his character and work acceptable and inspiring: his glory is intelligence; his attributes include justice and mercy; his purpose is to effect the immortality and eternal (or godlike) life of human beings. I like his name, our *Father*.

As I observe the order and beauty in nature and the intelligence and goodness in human nature, it is easier for me to believe that they are the product of an intelligent, self-conscious, ethical being than to believe that they have resulted from chance or from blind and impersonal sources.

I recognize that many aspects of life are not beautiful but cruel and involve much pain and suffering. My Mormon faith does not make God responsible for natural evil or for man's inhumanity to man, for God, too, must cope with uncreated, eternal elements and intelligences (see D&C 93).

I believe I have felt the influence of Deity in my life in answer to prayers and when involved in speaking, teaching, and working in their behalf. But I acknowledge that this feeling rests in part on faith.

If God exists, my faith in him will be all to my good. Should I perchance be mistaken, I have lost nothing by living with hope and faith in his attributes—intelligence, integrity, and love—for these represent life at its best.

MY FAITH IN CHRIST

I have never heard the voice of Christ, but I did have a remarkable personal experience of him. Early one morning, after a rather sleepless night during which I was struggling with what I perceived to be a serious problem, I lay awake in bed unable to find peace in any reasonable solution. Suddenly the Savior stood at the foot of my bed, his arms stretched out and a warm smile on his face. He gave me a wonderful feeling of peace and joy. Whether I merely dreamed that he came to me or he actually did is not as important to me as the feeling of acceptance I had.

I also know from adequate historical evidence that he lived. As with the Father, I am impressed by the character and teachings of those who have borne witness of him such as Isaiah, the authors of the Gospels, Paul, and Joseph Smith.

For me, the Savior is the world's greatest teacher, by word and example, of the values of life. His concern for people, his emphasis on humility, integrity, and love are inspiring. They are as meaningful for this life as they are for eternity. Jesus is my ideal and my inspiration.

Jesus has helped me to avoid some evils of life and inspired me to rise above others. He has spared me from setting my mind and heart on material values that don't satisfy and has made clear to me the things that matter most, that bring the deepest satisfaction.

Jesus is my hope and faith in eternal life. Without faith in immortality I would be sad; with it I am hopeful and glad. Again, should there be no immortality, I have lost nothing by my discipleship of Jesus. His way of life has value for here and now as well as for eternity. Even without believing in a hereafter, I would still try to follow Jesus' principles to make the most of my sojourn on earth.

MY FAITH IN IMMORTALITY

I have never seen or talked with anyone who once lived on earth and has moved on. My belief in immortality rests on faith. From a purely rational point of view, I agree with Socrates that death is either the best night's sleep a person ever had undisturbed by dreams, or one goes to a world where justice reigns and one may converse with people who have gone before (see Plato's *Apology*).

My faith in eternal life rests on several sources. (1) The witnesses of Jesus' resurrection as recorded in the New Testament and in Joseph Smith's teachings and experience, including the Book of Mormon. (2) A universe that can create the mind of human beings can, I believe, preserve it. (3) Living with the faith that life is eternal encourages me to live for lasting values and to think of my relationships with others as everlasting. (4) I find the faith that human beings are created in the image of God and can grow in his likeness motivating and exciting. If he exists eternally, so can we. (5) Should I be mistaken in my faith that life does not end with death, I have lost nothing in this life by living with the assurance of immortality and with an eternal perspective.

MY FAITH IN THE LDS CHURCH

My allegiance to The Church of Jesus Christ of Latter-day Saints rests on faith. I have not heard a divine voice telling me that the Church is of God. My faith in its divine origin and calling rests on more than eighty years of experience in the Church.

I grew up in a family devoted to religion and the Church. My mother was a devout, loyal Church member. My father, trained in philosophy, taught and exemplified the teachings of Jesus. He believed in the Fatherhood of God and the brotherhood of all men. He stressed the ethical principles of the gospel.

The LDS church provided a meaningful setting and influence for me in my growing up years in an early suburb of Salt Lake City. I had the same wonderful bishop, Elias S. Woodruff, from the time I was four years old until age twenty. He was reverent and spiritual, but also interested in the total welfare of individuals. He provided opportunities for young people to experience the joy of service and the value of belonging in a Christian fellowship.

I enjoyed my childhood and youth in the Church. It fulfilled many of my basic needs. It provided people who cared for me, friends and opportunities to serve, a faith that enabled me to feel my worth and gave purpose and meaning to my life. I was encouraged to express my faith in words and actions.

At twenty years of age I went to Germany and Switzerland on a mission for the Church. There I noted consciously for the first time what the Church and its teachings could do for the believer coming into a new way of life. The lay character of the Church proved especially helpful in integrating converts into a religious fellowship. I learned much about faith, humility, and love of God and man from those German and Swiss Saints. They helped me to appreciate the role of the Church in the religious life.

For twenty-eight years I worked with college students at an LDS Institute of Religion. My relationship with them was manifold and very rich for me. I taught classes, counseled, worshiped, dined and danced, and visited widows and the afflicted with students. I witnessed the beautiful fruits of the gospel and Church in the lives of students who were humble, had faith, and the commitment to serve in the Church. Their lives inspired me.

What is my faith in the Church today? It is my faith that Joseph Smith received divine authority (priesthood) to organize the church of Christ and administer the ordinances thereof and that he received revelations concerning Deity and human life that conform to reality. I feel comfortable with that faith and would encourage people to examine the same.

I respect everyone's right to believe and belong to whatever faith and church he or she wishes. I do not believe that we have in the LDS church any monopoly on knowledge or virtue. I know and admire many people, not of my faith and church, who are true disciples of Jesus and/or the prophets.

The Church exists for people, not people for the Church. The Church was established to help people become true followers of Jesus Christ. To the extent it succeeds, it fulfills its divine calling. I would rather be a good follower of Jesus outside the Church than an indifferent one in the Church.

CONCLUSION

Let me reiterate my theme: we can *know* the truth and value of the great religious-ethical principles Jesus taught. We must exercise, I believe, faith in some of the most basic questions of life: the existence of God, the mission of Jesus Christ, the immortality of the human soul, and the divine calling of the Church.

I like two definitions of faith: "Faith is the exceedingness of the possible over the real" (William James) and "Faith is reason grown courageous" (Sir Wilfred Grenfell). I have found living by faith based on experience to be most rewarding, fulfilling, and even adventurous.

Looking Back:
Reflections from Those Who Loved Him

Funeral Tributes to Lowell Bennion

Lowell Lindsay Bennion was born July 16, 1908 ,in Salt Lake City, Utah, and died there also on February 21, 1996. The East Millcreek Stake Center on February 26 was filled with more than 800 who came to pay tribute to the memory of this unique man.

Bishop Alan Barnes conducted the service. The family prayer at the closing of the casket was offered by Lowell's second son, Douglas C. Bennion, who is a teacher like his father. At the organ for prelude and postlude music was former Salt Lake Tabernacle organist Robert Cundick, who had called the family to say he would like to play for his friend Lowell.

Other music was offered with the same generosity of talent and spirit. Rebecca Bennion Glade, a niece, sang "Be Still and Know That I Am God," accompanied by Lowell and Merle's only daughter, Ellen B. Stone, an elementary school teacher, in whose home her parents lived for ten years and were lovingly cared for. Becky led the congregation in singing two of Lowell's favorite hymns, "Because I Have Been Given Much" and "I Stand All Amazed," accompanied by Robert Cundick. To conclude the service, Tom and Ellan Jeanne Pike, forever friends of the family, sang of what had been Lowell's focus in a life of believing and service, "O Divine Redeemer," again accompanied by Ellen B. Stone.

Naomi A. Bennion, a beautician and wife of Douglas, who had spent every morning for more than three years helping Merle and Lowell to be splendidly ready for their days, gave the invocation:

Heavenly Father, we're gathered at this time as friends and relatives of Lowell Bennion. We're indeed grateful for his life and for the role that he has played in all of our lives. May we strive to live the values that he has taught us. And we do ask a blessing on this service, that thy Spirit will be here, that it will be with those that participate and all those that are present. We now dedicate this meeting unto thee, and we say these things in the name of thy son Jesus Christ, Amen.

Lindsay R. Bennion, oldest grandchild of Lowell and Merle, now in a Ph. D. program in English in Indiana, spoke of his grandfather as he knew him at his Teton Boys Ranch. (Another "Lindsay," daughter of Ellen, had spoken at her grandmother's funeral.)

TRIBUTE TO OPA

Good afternoon.

It is wonderful to see all of you here on such a snowy winter's day. Our family is touched by this showing of love for my grandfather.

I'm here representing the grandkids—who my grandfather would have referred to as a "fine bunch." You are a fine bunch and I know that Oma and Opa were very proud of you. [The grandkids called Grandma and Grandpa Bennion "Oma" and "Opa" after the German custom.]

As I prepared for today and reflected on Opa's life and works, I realized that some of my cousins and siblings didn't get to spend a lot of time with Opa. So, I'd like to share a few of my memories of Opa from a grandson's perspective.

This chapel and the surrounding neighborhood bring back a lot of memories of when we lived next door to Oma and Opa, but it's too cold and snowy here today for this occasion. I'd like to move this gathering to a more appropriate spot—one of Opa's favorites. For the next few minutes I'd like you to come with me to Teton Valley.

There is a beautiful ranch in the southwest foothills where national forest meets fields and pastures. It's a warm Sunday afternoon in August and the smell of the mountain air is indescribable. As we walk up a dirt road from the A-frame, we can turn and look across the valley and see three of the peaks of the Grand Teton Range.

Opa—we called him "Doc" at the ranch—is walking up ahead of us. He's wearing his jeans and work shoes, but still has his Sunday shirt on from attending church with the good people of the Victor Ward a few hours earlier.

Past the tack house and corral to our left, and through the fields where alfalfa bales are drying in the sun, we walk to the edge of an aspen and pine forest. A few steps into a small grove of lodgepole pines is a clearing with benches made from split logs. At the front is a pine podium. This is the "chapel in the pines." Opa created it as a place where the boys and counselors could contemplate and express the things that matter most. His invitation to us this afternoon is to think about someone we admire or who has influenced our lives. In this setting, I feel more comfortable sharing my feelings about Opa. For me, Opa and the ranch are inextricably tied together.

I did not know him as an institute teacher, university professor, administrator, or director of the Community Services Council—as many of you knew him. To me Opa was a gardener and a rancher. He ran a ranch where he could organize work and give boys good experiences. As I got older, I became aware of him as a writer and a guide to studying the gospel.

When I was six or seven, Opa took me to the ranch with him for a week. We bunked together in the shack that was jokingly referred to as the "executive mansion." One morning we woke to the sound of mice running around on the floor. He helped me set traps and paid me a nickel for each mouse that I caught. That was his bounty for mice. Fifteen years later—the last time I was a counselor at the ranch—the price of mice was still a nickel. This is indicative of the timeless quality of the ranch experience. It didn't matter whether you attended the ranch in the '60s, '70s, or '80s, the core experiences of learning to take satisfaction in hard work, enjoying recreation and fellowship in the outdoors, and being mentally stimulated by discussions and debates never changed.

As with so many of Opa's projects, he identified a few of the things that he thought would most benefit others, then created an environment and opportunity where it could happen. The ranch experience continues and I am grateful—as I'm sure Opa was—to those who are making it possible. I hope to send my children to the ranch someday.

I don't think I fully appreciated living next door to Oma and Opa as a boy. I became a convenient source of labor for Opa's garden behind the house. Working with Opa in the garden did give me a profound respect for manure. Every fall, he would acquire truckloads of it from one of his prized suppliers and we would spread it out over the whole garden. It was the same thing with his garden at the ranch. Opa loved the rich soil, manure for fertilizer, and his irrigation turn. Most of all, he loved sharing the produce from his gardens with those in need.

Opa made it a point to talk with me and many other boys and counselors on the long drive between the ranch and Salt Lake City. We made the trip together in vehicles of varying degrees of reliability and comfort, but it didn't matter to Opa. As with his gardening, he made the most of a drive by turning it into an opportunity to work with and uplift those around him.

Opa's love for work and service was contagious. I still picture him standing on the back deck of the A-frame lodge, the sun coming up over the Tetons. He had a clipboard of work assignments and would divide the boys and counselors up into teams for the morning's work. He loved those mornings at the ranch, teaching us how to tend the garden, tamp a fence post into the ground so that it was solid, or paint a building.

In later years, when I was at college and our visits were less frequent, I began to know Opa through his writings. I would come up for a visit, hoping he could give me some guidance on some decision I was trying to make. But I could never get him to tell me what I should do. As those of you who have ever sought his counsel know, Opa would never tell you what he thought you should do. Instead he would get you talking. He taught and counseled as the Savior must have, through probing questions and a listening ear.

After he got me feeling better about my life and decisions, he would build my confidence by talking to me about his writing. He would say, "I have an idea that I think would make a nice little book," then ask me what I thought. Other times he would ask me to read a draft that he was working on. Opa had excellent readers and editors and certainly did not need my opinion. But he knew how it would make me feel to be included in his work.

At some point, I realized that when Opa was younger than I am now, he decided that what was most important in life was to follow the Savior. He determined that the best way to do that was to serve others, both spiritually and temporally, then spent the rest of his life in that pursuit. As a natural extension of his work, he created opportunities for others to join him in serving.

Even though we have not been able to spend as much time with Opa as we would like, his work and his influence will continue through us. I am grateful to Eugene England and Mary Bradford, whose efforts to compile his writings and describe his life will make it so much easier to remember Opa and teach my children about him. I am so grateful to Ellen, Howard, my dad, Naomi, Lindsay, and Jacob who took such loving care of Oma and Opa these past years. I know there were also many other family members and friends who cared for them. We're grateful to you.

As I look out at all of you, I see a community of people who have been influenced by Opa. It is difficult to express how it touches our family to know how you feel about him. I think it would please Opa most if, before we leave the chapel in the pines today, we would each reflect on things that matter most in life and recommit to following Jesus Christ through service and love.

I say these things in the name of Jesus Christ, Amen.

Lowell C. (Ben) Bennion, Merle and Lowell's oldest son, a professor of geography at Humboldt State University in California, spoke of his father as remembered by his brothers and sisters and children.

A CELEBRATION OF THE LIFE OF LOWELL L. BENNION

Lindsay Bennion and I share a mixed blessing in bearing one of Opa's Father's names and in being the oldest of our respective generations. That double burden places us in the challenging position of representing the rest of the family. I just pray that I may do as well as Lindsay has done.

Someone has said that no two siblings have the same parents. That seems particularly true in a family like ours with six children spread out over nearly twenty years. Each of us, like each of you, has known Mom and Dad in a different way. To summarize the nature of our family's diversity, let me share with you some words I wrote:

The clearest sign of Lowell and Merle's individuality lies in the utter diversity of their offspring. No two of them resemble each other, either physically or socially (as you may have noticed while greeting us in the viewing line prior to this service). We vary greatly in complexion, stature, and personality. . . . Our parents set high standards for us but never rejected us when we fell short. The two of them differed as much as we do, making me wonder at times what drew and held them together. Dad, a product of early suburban Salt Lake, always yearned for a farm or ranch; Mom, an orphan from Uintah County, clung to the city once she discovered it as a teenager. Yet they developed strong bonds of love and respect that endured to the end of their sixty-six-year marriage (and which are now being renewed, we hope).

To summarize the family's feelings about Father and to paint a verbal picture of him, I have asked his surviving siblings and children—four of each (not counting me)—what they would have me say. And this is what they, grouped by order of age, more or less, said.

Uncle Lynn referred to Lowell as a "great man" and recalled all the books he wrote, writings that demonstrate his unusual ability to balance faith and reason with humanism at its best.

Uncle Grant described Dad as "one of a kind, one whom I've admired all my life." Stranded in Hawaii this week, Grant had a neighbor fax me a copy of the tales with which he [Grant] regaled the family on the occasion of Dad's eightieth birthday and the Folks' sixtieth wedding anniversary. Let me share just one of the stories with you as a sample of his delightful humor:

As a youngster, Lowell received much sympathy after being belted in the face by his pony Black Beauty's shod hoof. He narrowly missed losing an eye, but not everyone knew he had invited the injury. To impress a girl his own age, he had clung to the pony's tail as they trotted around the corral. To hasten the pace he poked her with a sharp stick, and she replied in kind. A few years later, Lowell met and married Merle Colton, a happy event for all of us and in keeping with the family need to upgrade itself through fortunate marriages—a pattern well established by Claire, Maurine, and Lynn.

Aunt Frances thought that Lowell always responded to others' needs, including her own. He seldom replied to her long and frequent letters, but once when she felt discouraged, she got an immediate and helpful response. To me her comment almost implies that Lowell might neglect someone who in his eyes had no particular need. The needy often caught his attention and concern before family and friends, for, after all, "They that are whole have no need of the physician" (Mark 2:17).

Uncle Vaughan described Lowell as "a real saint, one of his heroes." Vaughn's appreciation of him increased when he and his wife Lyle decided to build a cabin at the Targhee, or opposite, end of Teton Valley from Dad's ranch. When his new neighbors learned he was Lowell's kid brother, they went out of their way to help him solve sundry building problems.

Brother Doug remembered well Dad's definition of *recreation*—refreshment of the mind or body by means of play, but only after a Saturday morning of hard labor hauling something like neighbor John Ungricht's fragrant chicken manure. After Doug and Dad had collected food for the Food Bank one morning, Dad suggested they go home for a drink of cool apple cider. Down they went into the cellar with their glasses. After filling them, they sat back and too a big drink of what turned out to be unadulterated cider vinegar.

Brother Steve emphasized the fact that before, during, and after his long tenure as a teacher Dad was "a man of the soil"—a would-be farmer and rancher. That's why for five years our family of seven drove around in that old red Chevy truck, usually with two boys (Steve and Doug) in the back. Steve thinks that earthy experience must account in part for Father's unusual ability to reach and teach people of every imaginable background and persuasion.

Brother Howard would encourage all of us—each in our own way—to continue Dad's tradition of trying to translate the rhetoric of religion into the practical realm of helping others. Howard probably would quote with approval a statement attributed to Saint Bernard of Clairvaux by Sister Elaine Jack [in the latest *Ensign*]: "If you are to do the work of a prophet, what you need is not a scepter but a hoe." Certainly both Howard and Doug's wife Naomi have shown us the real meaning of "tender loving care" while tending Dad and Mom the past few years.

My sister Ellen, who with the assistance of her children, Lindsay and Jacob, assumed the lion's share of the burden of caring for our parents, expressed the view that everything Dad did had to have a purpose. He confessed to her more than once that he felt driven by what he saw as people's most pressing needs and had to act to meet them if he could. That feeling accounts for his fondness for the Hindu teaching: "To action alone hast thou a right, not to its fruits." Ellen also asked me to single out four individuals for special thanks, people who came almost weekly to see Father during his final year, even though he could hardly converse with them. Fred Buchanan came and read to him; Mindy Probst played her violin for him; Duwayne Schmidt took him for short visits to others; Clyde Reavely visited and often ran errands for him. Together these four helped lessen Ellen's stress considerably.

To this family portrait of Father I would also like add the views of two individuals to represent the ward, stake, and neighborhood. The first voice dates from the distant past, when East Millcreek consisted mainly of small homes on large large lots rather than huge houses on tiny plots. Bryant S. Hinckley [President Hinckley's father] lived on what is now Craig Drive, but he was our nearest neighbor to the south. We like to think he had Father in mind when he wrote:

"I have a farm neighbor who is beloved by all who know him. He is a professional man of eminence in the field of education, whose hands are calloused with hard work, whose mind is a source of light and inspiration to both old and young, and whose life is an expression of Christian behavior which makes him pre-eminent among his associates. When you talk with this man you learn something, and when you live near him, your faith in mankind is increased."

The second voice belongs to that of one of my in-laws' neighbors who left us a card last evening with this sentiment: "Brother Bennion doesn't need a headstone—he left monuments all around us with the Boys Ranch, the Bennion Center at the U, and all the Community Services Council groups."

Have any of you wondered what Father himself would want added to this portrait? I asked him that question soon after Mother's funeral [September 30, 1994] when he first told me he would like me to speak at his. As best we can remember, this is what he told my wife Sherry and me. "I believe I have honored the charge President David O. McKay gave me soon after my appointment as first director of the LDS Institute at the U. 'Be true to yourself and loyal to the cause.'" Dad said, "I believe I've kept my integrity and stayed loyal to my church and culture." For him, integrity did not preclude loyalty or vice-versa. To understand how he balanced those two when, on occasion, they conflicted, you may want to scan one or both of the two books Lindsay mentioned—the efforts of Eugene England and Mary Bradford to place Dad's writings and life in context and thereby increase our appreciation of him. In any case, Lowell felt whole, not holy, and that wholeness enlarged his capacity to love.

Finally, what would "Gentle Ben"—the other Lowell Bennion—add to this family painting? Not much, rest assured, for already I can hear both Dad and Ellen telling me I've talked long enough. But I would like to share with you the only short summary I know of that captures much of Father's philosophy of life. I call it his "Learn to Like. . ." creed and have taken the liberty of editing a little these lines that appear in both the England and Bradford books:

> Learn to like reading, conversation, music.
>
> Learn to like plain food, plain service, plain cooking.
>
> Learn to like people, though many of them may be different from you.
>
> Learn to like work and enjoy the satisfaction of doing it as well as you can.
>
> Learn to like the songs of birds, the companionship of pets.
>
> Learn to like gardening, puttering around the house, and fixing things.
>
> Learn to like the sunrise and sunset, the beating or rain on the roof and windows, the gentle fall of snow on a winter day.
>
> Learn to keep your wants simple and refuse to be controlled by the likes and dislikes of others.

That last line expresses so well the Bennion tendency which Dad inherited that made him almost as independent as a coyote. The line, however, that epitomizes him best in my mind's eye is the third one. Lowell Bennion learned to like people and, to an uncommon degree, loved to serve them, no matter who they were. His compulsion to serve, driven by his desire to be a disciple of Christ, meant that his long-suffering wife and impatient children had to learn to share him with others—with all of you and many others.

Let me share with you three examples of Dad's compulsion to serve. So far as I know, Dad never took time to climb nearby Mount Olympus, his favorite mountain. He never went hiking with any of us children unless it involved a group of institute students or boys from the Teton Valley Ranch. Not too long after Sherry and I moved to Humboldt County, California, in 1970, Mom and Dad decided to pay us a week-long visit. We spent little of that time walking in the redwoods or collecting agates on the beaches because Dad, not I, insisted that we paint our A-frame house. In recent years we have watched with amazement (and amusement) as Father visited and tried to assist others who were in better health than he.

It took us a long while, but when we finally realized we could not curb, much less cure, Lowell's compulsive behavior, Mother and we children somehow learned to accept it and adjust our living to his life of service. If we could add just one line to Dad's creed, it would be: "Learn to like to relax and recreate for its own sake." I might even suggest that those of you who know Ellen think twice before asking her to do something, since she shares some of Father's compulsion and has not yet learned to say "no" to requests for help.

In his long life of serving others, Lowell Bennion learned to believe that all the Lord required of him (or us) is "to do justly, and to love mercy, and to walk humbly with thy God" (Micah 6:8). May we honor our father, grandfather, and friend by learning in our way how we can best do the same, I pray in the name of Jesus Christ, our Divine Redeemer, Amen.

Emma Lou Thayne, long-time friend of both Lowell and Merle, spoke as representative of the thousands who had been influenced by the life of this man.

LOWELL BENNION FUNERAL TRIBUTE

Today, driving here in the snowstorm that seemed so inopportune for a funeral, I wondered if this would keep many people away. And then I thought, Oh no, not for Lowell, not ever. What could keep any of us away? And I thought too about a saying that my mother calligraphied thirty years ago and that's been on our bulletin board forever:

The majesty of calm: Advice is like the snow. The softer it falls the longer it stays and the deeper it sinks into the mind.—Coleridge.

Perfect. For Lowell, for this day of remembering him.

Emerson said, "I can't remember the books I've read any more than the meals I've eaten; even so, they have made me." In like fashion, I would like to say, "Lowell, I can't remember the truths you've taught me any more than the air I've breathed; even so, my going is alive with light and warmth because of them. And so is the going of how many out there today?

In Matthew 22:36 lay the light and truth for Lowell. When the lawyer asked the Master "which is the great commandment in the law? Jesus said unto him, Thou shalt love the Lord thy God with all thy heart, and with all thy soul, and with all thy mind. . . . And the second is like unto it, Thou shalt love thy neighbour as thyself. On these two commandments hang all the law and the prophets." And there they hung for Lowell.

This was his *vertical* and *horizontal* approach to religion and to living. Imagine two lines, one coming down, one going across, intersecting. One going up, the other across, and he at the crux of both, going in both directions at the same time all of his life. He moved along each line as easily as he did from work to play to worship at his boys ranch, there in the Tetons. And he invited all of us to go along with him. I, like you, have gone. From his classes at the institute as a sixteen-year-old freshman at the university, to touring Israel with him as guide for my husband and me and three teenage daughters forty-five years later. Then along to teach from his lesson manuals, to later write them under his guidance, to read his books and articles, 120 and more, over the years. To hear him speak—I remember when [my husband and I] were dating, there used to be listed in the Saturday night paper the speakers that were going to appear on Sunday night at Sacrament meetings. We'd look to see who was up, and if Lowell Bennion was somewhere, we were there.

How many places has he spoken, at farewells and gatherings and funerals? Always he was willing to be where anybody asked him to be. And to consult with us. Always I've gone to him to say, What do you think, Lowell? I wanted him to be in on the lives of others, like when he helped me teach in Relief Society about service or officiate in the exchange of rings (not part of the temple ceremony) for our fourth daughter, Dinny, and Mike Trabert, whose parents could not go to the temple to see them married. Lowell was the one who could make it right for everybody, his advice to them as gentle as any falling snow.

I wonder, Lowell, do you know how loved you are? Basic to your life, as Ben has said, has been that reciprocity with people. We've heard from his family, Lindsay and Ben, and out there are all of you students and fellow workers, colleagues, ward member, neighbors, members of boards and committees, writers of manuals, diggers in the soil, Teton Ranch boys grown into men, counselors, friends in a twenty-five-year-old Lowell Bennion study group, cousins, the Bennion Center volunteers, ranchers, educators, artists, scholars, doctors, lawyers, merchants, chiefs, so many of us who have been recipients of his gifts. And then all of you who have visited him, taken him for rides, read to him, who've stayed part of his life and he part of yours. Ellen said he would have liked a funeral to hear from each of you who wanted to say something. He would want to listen to see how *we* are. How many eons might that take?

For me, it's been more than fifty years of his being my counselor and friend. Why do we love him? Foremost, because he has never failed us. This complex man was as consistent as the seasons. And as immediate. Even as he revered the past and the wisdom of the ages, his purview was the present. For instance, in our valley today, in the throes of contention, charges and countercharges, I can see Lowell as he's always been, at that meeting place of the vertical and the horizontal. Tossed on a sea of divisiveness, rowing quietly, he would bring disparate views and hostile people to see the things that matter most and to know that they would not be at the mercy of the things that matter least. He would be asking, What is the overall good? Not *whose* idea, but *what* idea might be best for all. His gift.

He was called on to represent the best in Mormonism across boundaries of race, age, situations, station, and persuasion. For example, at a diversity conference a few years ago sponsored by Westminster College, two hundred women met, as different as trees in a forest, together for two days. At one session in the legislative chambers at the Capitol, Governor Scott Matheson opened and Dr. Lowell Bennion closed. Lowell talked about service and healing and how to offer both, about how the government and people could help each other.

After his talk that day, I walked out with Esther Landa, recent past president of the National Council of Jewish Women. She said to me, "I want to belong to his church." Of course this was not literal; what she meant was that there was with Lowell a meeting of heart and mind. And she said another thing to me, "Now we're not just a conference, we are a congregation."

Wherever Lowell expressed himself, a gathering could become a congregation, but the last thing he wanted in the world was to be sought out as a head of anything. He didn't want a "following." He wanted listeners to find themselves and the divine in whatever he had to offer. To find their own potential for good. On the vertical and the horizontal. And then to show it, to act on it. To operate always from strength instead of weakness, to be actors, not reactors.

Love, Lowell said, is an active verb. He moved with it in every direction, up, down, across—and took us in. How? Because he was basically a happy person, the best thing any of us has to offer. Because he was happy—and that's not as a mood, but as a mode—he could forget himself and then think not of what was happening for him, but what was happening for others.

On one of the last times that I was with him, I said, "Lowell, do you have any idea how many people you've influenced? With that smile that had carved itself into his face so that he was smiling even if he wasn't smiling he said, "I never had time to think about that." Neither did he have time to complain or stagnate or tread in the murky waters of antagonism or blame or accusation. He never had to put anyone else down in order to raise himself. Self-pity was not part of this man. Impaired as he in later years seemed to be, he never lost that spark.

And probably, Lowell, it came to you naturally, through genes and those you grew up with. Oh, the Bennions I've known! Double cousin to Lowell, LaVon Bennion Cannon, who was my mother's dearest friend from first grade, said to me one day about herself and Lowell, "We don't hate people. We don't criticize, we analyze. We never get depressed; we were born happy and stayed that way."

Lowell's mother, Clara, whom my mother loved, at ninety-five had been widowed for twenty years and was still living alone. One night the power went out. She had a call from her daughter Maureen saying, "Mother shall I come pick you up?" Her mother answered, "I'm fine. I've lighted a candle and I'll play my guitar." At ninety-five. Lowell's father, Milton Bennion, a noted educator, before the time of insulin had to have his leg amputated below the knee because of diabetes and gangrene. His response: "Well, if I'm going to die by inches, I'd rather die feet first than head first."

That's how it happened for Lowell, feet first. His balance left him, but never his head. The last time I walked down that hallway at Ellen's home to see him about two weeks ago, I could not help noticing a gaping hole in the wall about eighteen inches above the floor, as if a lead basketball had been thrown through it. It's where he'd fallen. Falls were common, getting more common. Parkinson's was having its way with him. On his head were healing blotches, often scabs. His eyes that day were black and blue, his nose swollen. He had been reading from a book flat on the table that he didn't have to hold. He had to turn his shoulders upward to see me as he sat at his table. But as I sat next to him, there was that light, alive still in his intense blue eyes. Naomi, gentle taker of care with him, asked, "Do you want your glasses off, Opa?" as she lifted them off for him to visit with me. Oh my, Naomi and Howard, Ellen, Lindsay [his granddaughter], and Jake, what you've done over this time to keep him home, as you did with your mother, so that they would never have to leave and be anywhere but home. What tender care, tender, tender care.

Merle said that his head was never still, even when he might have been sleeping. It never was. Right to the end, not that I saw. Thinking about that head together with his so active heart, I think about the sacrifices his family made in the interest of both. It had to be hard along the way to realize that he was about his Father's business. His Father's, all of ours. It's easy for anybody who is about public, Church, or other business, especially someone called as Lowell was to think like Golda Meier, "Who or what have I neglected today?" That must run through every other effort.

Central to his pyramid of values were learning and integrity. I can see him walking into a classroom face first and hands second, but with his head and heart and spirit always aligned. Because he stayed whole, he was always learning, right to the end. One time only a few months ago, he told me he had read the Book of Mormon in two days. His favorites were Ammon and Mosiah and Nephi, II Nephi. Once I asked him what his favorite scripture was, and of course it would always be "Do justly and love mercy and walk humbly with thy Lord" from Micah. But that day he opened his worn leather four-in-one, the Bible, Book of Mormon, Doctrine and Covenants and Pearl of Great Price, with hands that wouldn't work for anything else and turned instantly to where he wanted to be. (Ellen said she envied him, that he'd had forty years to study the scriptures as a profession.) This day he read to me what of course he knew by heart: "And the Lord shall come to recompense unto every man according to his work and measure to every man according to the measure which he has measured to his fellow man." And in II Nephi: ". . . and none were forbidden." Not unlike his forever "Neither do I condemn thee." He never lost sight of the big picture or the worth of every soul.

Little wonder the Community Services Center, the Food Bank, the Bennion Center at the U, with Irene Fisher to direct it as he would, and a Lowell Bennion study group that will continue to learn, hoping not to fade into the "arrogance of ignorance." No wonder his favorite hymns have just been sung, "Because I Have Been Given Much, I Too Must Give" and "I Know That My Redeemer Lives." The horizontal, the vertical, right there in those two hymns.

Yes, he lived in the present, in day-tight compartments. In that last visit that I had with him not long ago, I asked him, "How are you, Lowell?" Typically he would answer, "Tolerably well." This time it was, "Rocky." He could put a simple, uncomplaining spin even on suffering. Where he hurt, how he hurt, he never said, even to those taking such gentle care of him. His life-long stance had been not to be defeated twice, once by circumstance and again by self. Instead, he would remember during the hardest defeat of his life seeing Christ at the foot of his bed, his arms out in welcome. He knew he was all right.

As disease crippled and limited his body, three fingers on his left hand refused to open. They curled into his palm. As we sat at his table, he asked me one time if I would try to open them. Those hands that had been so rugged and so full of giving and offering blessings, the great big hands were now reduced to tendons and bones and an almost empty palm. But as I worked with those fingers and rubbed, we often talked about Merle, dear to both of us.

The next to last time I was with him, as I was working on his fingers on his left hand, he struggled to get his other hand up, and then began to rub *my* hand, across the top, down the fingers, as we were talking. I thought, at eighty-seven, however impaired, at heart he is still intact. I asked him, "Lowell, what would you give me as advice today?" As quick as he'd always been, he said, "Keep your own voice and write with your own pen." Of course I thought, Lowell, that's what you've done, that's what I would love to do.

Today, I give this poem to you, my friend, this about your being home.

ON BEING HOME

Your wondering is over,
You are alive as in your belief.
A radiance has taken you.
Now part of the council of all beings
You are exuberant as the earth in the cosmos
Alive, astonishing, beyond maps
And places to fall.

No invader disease, foreign and presumptious
Can have its way.
Nothing is now too late

Or to be demolished.
Your awakening is unbounded
Pure surprise.

The Light
Over, around, suffuses your coming
As your passing wrenches us all
Through the flailings of our endangered species

To where sleep and beyond
Beckon from birth
And feather the heaviest death
With luminous fingers
To draw us
Weeping with the lightness of being
Home.

No, I cannot remember all the truths you have taught me, Lowell, any more than the books I've read and the meals I've eaten; even so, they have made me. For the vertical and the horizontal, Lowell, thank you. Thank you for that and for offering me ways to understand your forever companion, Jesus Christ. In his name, Amen.

President Gordon B. Hinckley, president of The Church of Jesus Christ of Latter-day Saints, a friend and once neighbor of Lowell, was the concluding speaker.

He paid tribute to Lowell and his late wife Merle as "just good people" and honored Lowell as a modern-day Good Samaritan. According to the Deseret News *account, President Hinckley noted that shining through all his "remarkable life and his writings" is a "testimony and conviction of the Lord Jesus Christ, the Son of God."*

The Salt Lake Tribune *reported that as he surveyed all the cars in the packed church parking lot for Dr. Bennion's funeral, he thought to himself, "Lowell Bennion never drove a car as good as the poorest of these." He reminisced about Lowell Bennion's penchant for old cars and trucks. To him, President Hinckley said, "a car was just a means to get somewhere to do good."*

"His methods," he said of Lowell, "sometimes were unorthodox, but his ends were 100% orthodox. Lifting people, encouraging people, helping people, and loving people."

From the Church News *report, "The central figure of his life was the Redeemer of the world. That was the root of his strength. That was the theme of his life. And he lived as he believed." The story went on, "President Hinckley said that Brother Bennion's objectives were lifting people, helping people, encouraging people, turning their lives around when they were headed in the wrong direction, giving encouragement in times of despair—comforting and blessing."*

The benediction was offered by Howard W. Bennion, youngest of four sons of Lowell and Merle, whose affection his father was able to reciprocate most visibly in his final months in the mutual exchange of professional and patient.

Our dear and kind Father in Heaven, What a blessing to be a part of Lowell Bennion's life. If we can do something that he would want, I believe more than anything, it would be to serve our fellowmen, to practice, to do, to actually be caregivers. We're going to miss him a lot. We're so grateful for this beautiful, beautiful service.

He has a great progeny, strong, beautiful. We're so appreciative of all those who have contributed to his care, have shown love and devotion. Father in Heaven, all your children mean so much to the family. We know he's rejoicing with Mother, and of course we feel that she probably said, "So I see you've kept me waiting again!" I'm sure they're both happy to be with our sister.

We're most grateful for the things that he has taught us, given to us, this truly Christlike man, who walked and did good all of his life. May thy Spirit and thy Son comfort and guide us, show us things to do, help us to carry on his example through work. We believe in this Church, and he was truly one of the chosen children.

We ask that thy Spirit be with us. Travel with us on this day. Although it's a beautiful day, let us use caution that we might rejoice again with our dear loved ones. We say these things humbly in Jesus' name, Amen.

Dedication of the grave was offered by Steven D. Bennion, educator and third son of Lowell and Merle, who shares his father's love of learning and positive involvement with people.